'*Stronger Together* is an insightful look into the inner world of world-class teams and how they came to be that way. Rhetoric- and pontification-free, this is a serious study of team dynamics proven to work and applicable to us all'

Brendan Hall, victorious Clipper Round the World
Yacht Race skipper and author of *Team Spirit*

'It gives me great pleasure to endorse Simon Hartley's latest book. It is simple to read and yet excellent for anybody looking to improve themselves. Simon engages you, he makes you think, he makes you reflect and, more importantly, gives you the confidence to act. As a coach working in international sport I find Simon's help supportive, simple and yet always appropriate'

Paul Farbrace, assistant coach, England Cricket

'*Stronger Together* is Simon Hartley at his brilliant best. Simple, usable messages that anyone in any team, business or organisation can practically implement to improve and get better every day. What I love about this book is there are searching questions that you can ask about yourself and your team, coupled with steps to help you turn the lessons into actions that make a real difference. Simon has had a real impact in making our team perform at a higher level and I challenge anyone not to be better for having read this book'

Toby Babb, managing director, Harrington Starr

'Thought-provoking stuff from a master of his subject. Required reading for anyone interested in teams, performance and sustained success. Invaluable'

James Kerr, author of *Legacy*

'*Stronger Together* will give you a unique view into the inner workings of world-class teams. Simon Hartley turns these into simple, powerful and practical lessons that you can apply to your own team. Reading this book really could help you to create an exceptional team'

Nigel McMinn, managing director, Lookers plc

'It is a rare talent that can take complex ideas and concepts of elite sporting performance and present them in a simple, accessible and engaging manner. Simon Hartley is such a talent. He has generously shared the benefits and wisdom of his hard-earned experiences, making a significant difference to sporting – and corporate – athletes alike, and produced a compelling page-turner. I cannot recommend it highly enough'

Professor Damian Hughes, the Liquid Thinker

STRONGER TOGETHER

HOW GREAT TEAMS WORK

SIMON HARTLEY

piatkus

To my lovely wife and gorgeous daughters –
you are the centre of my world.

PIATKUS

First published in Great Britain in 2015 by Piatkus

1 3 5 7 9 10 8 6 4 2

A CIP catalogue record for this book
is available from the British Library.

ISBN 978-0-349-40848-4

Typeset in Stone Serif and Futura by M Rules
Printed and bound in Great Britain by
Clays Ltd, St Ives plc

Papers used by Piatkus are from well-managed forests
and other responsible sources.

MIX
Paper from
responsible sources
FSC® C104740

Piatkus
An imprint of
Little, Brown Book Group
Carmelite House
50 Victoria Embankment
London EC4Y 0DZ

An Hachette UK Company
www.hachette.co.uk

www.piatkus.co.uk

About the author

Simon Hartley is a globally respected sport psychology consultant and performance coach. He helps athletes and business people to get their mental game right. For almost 20 years, Simon has worked with gold medallists, world record holders, world champions, top five world-ranked professional athletes and championship-winning teams. He has worked at the highest level of sport, including spells in Premiership football, Premiership rugby union, First Class County Cricket, Super League, Formula One, professional golf and tennis, as well as with international teams and Team GB Olympians.

The year 2011 saw the publication of Simon's first book, *Peak Performance Every Time*, which was followed in 2012 by *How to Shine*, and in 2013 by *Two Lengths of the Pool. Could I Do That?* and *How to Herd Cats* were published in 2014.

For almost ten years, Simon has also applied the principles of sport psychology to business, education, healthcare and the charity sector. This has included projects with some of the world's leading corporations and foremost executives. He is also an international professional speaker, delivering keynotes throughout the world.

For more information on Simon, please visit www.be-world-class.com

Contents

Preface

What is it that differentiates the greatest teams in the world? What sets them apart and separates them from their competition? What do they have that other teams don't have? What do they do that other teams don't do?

These questions have intrigued me for years. As a sport psychology consultant and performance coach, I have spent almost 20 years helping elite sports teams to increase their performance. Unsurprisingly, much of my time is focused on helping them develop teamwork. Interestingly, the same is true when I work with individual performers, such as golfers, swimmers or track-and-field athletes. Although they may compete on their own, these athletes are acutely aware that their team has a massive impact on their success. Most elite-level athletes have a support team, which includes coaches, sports scientists and sports medics. The athletes know that, despite the fact that they compete on their own, theirs is a team sport.

I have come to realise that sport is a team game. I'd also argue that business is a team game. In fact, I'd go further and propose that *life* is a team game. The ability to be a great team player is something that pervades many areas of life – not just sport or, indeed, work. These principles underpin our ability to work together, whether it's through a profession, voluntary group, social group or even our family. Therefore, understanding how to develop a great team is incredibly valuable to us all.

Several years ago I set out on a quest: to understand how world-class teams work and how they're created. To answer my questions, I've studied a range of teams that are among the very best in the world in their chosen field. I am curious to know what common characteristics they share and how they have developed great teamwork. My rationale is simple. If there are characteristics that are found in world-class sports teams, Special Forces units, the world's best aerobatic display team, surgical teams, yacht crews, and even great animal teams, these characteristics might well be generic. Principles that exist in such diverse disciplines are therefore likely to translate into almost any field.

This book is the culmination of my own experiences and discoveries, combined with thoughts and reflections from my time with world-class teams. I have sought to understand what differentiates these phenomenal teams and what qualities they all share. Doing this allows us to understand the core principles and how to apply them to others. As well as presenting my perspective, I have made a conscious effort to give you a window into these teams. I have deliberately tried to lift the lid so that you can peer inside. The leaders whom I have met have inspired me. Their words are incredibly insightful. As twice-Michelin-starred chef Kenny Atkinson once told me, 'Let the ingredients speak for themselves.' Therefore, where possible, I have left many of these leaders' accounts in a raw state so that you can read their words too. These insights give us a unique glimpse into the minds of world-class team members and their leaders, and they help to illustrate how these people think.

Over the years, I have worked with some of the greatest sports teams in the world: World Championship and European Championship winners. These experiences have helped me to understand what's required to develop a team capable of leading the world, but of course there is always more to learn. My journey, working with and studying these amazing teams, has been incredible. I have learned more about teams, teamwork and leadership than I ever thought possible. Personally, I have found the experience transformational. I truly hope that you gain as much value and inspiration as I have.

Acknowledgements

I would like to offer my sincere thanks to everyone who has contributed to this book. In particular, I am incredibly grateful to those who have given their time, offered their insights and shared their experiences with me. Thank you:

Former SAS major, Floyd Woodrow, MBE

Former Red Arrows team leader, Jas Hawker

Clipper Round the World Yacht Race skipper and author of *Team Spirit*, Brendan Hall

FIFA World Cup referee, Howard Webb

Lotus Formula One Race team manager, Paul Seaby

Sri Lanka's World Cup-winning cricket coach, Paul Farbrace

Former America's Cup helmsman, Andy Beadsworth

Three-time America's Cup-winning sailor, and Ben Ainslie Racing's sailing manager, Jono MacBeth

The Boxer Rebellion's drummer, Piers Hewitt

Author of *Legacy*, James Kerr

Biologist Dr Dan Franks, from the University of York

They are all fantastic people who have shared their thoughts and wisdom freely.

I am grateful to Brendon Burchard for his permission to use his characteristics of great leaders, the 'six Es'. I also offer thanks to Sir Ian McGeechan for writing the Foreword, and to the team at Piatkus and Little, Brown for all their help in publishing this book.

I am forever grateful to my friends and family, who are a constant source of support and guidance.

Finally, thank you for reading this book. I hope that it gives as much insight and inspiration as it has given me.

Foreword

I have been lucky and privileged to have been involved with some outstanding teams. Outstanding teamwork, for me, creates the ultimate environment in which to work.

Great teams often evolve when like-minded, committed people create – through honesty and trust – an environment where minds remain open and ideas are accepted as an essential part of development. What they also create is a powerful lead-support system in which strengths are recognised and responsibility can shift depending on the skill and knowledge needed.

I have found that great teams challenge their members to keep pushing the boundaries of their individual performances, but they also have an acute awareness of a collective intelligence which drives the team's performance. There is an understanding of the mixture of strengths and talent needed to create and sustain a truly outstanding performance environment. It is not about everyone being the same, but understanding the complementary strengths needed for consistently successful outcomes.

Great teams also know where responsibilities lie at any one moment, and those taking the lead are clear about their own role in delivering, as I call them, 'world-class basics', i.e. under pressure, delivering what they are good at so that someone else can then come into play with their strengths.

For me, it is like having an operational time-line in which all team members know where they are, who is responsible and what comes next – a 'cause-and-effect' understanding of every action. This, I believe, leads to the big-result outcome, and to get this we need to review and assess every day. I always believe improvements can be made individually but also with an understanding of the impact they will have on the overall result, as well as on someone else's performance. Everyone then understands the value of their own contribution, as well as its overall impact.

In sport, the on-field performance and the result are there for all to see, but equally important is the chemistry and performance of the off-field support group and the standards by which they operate. If this is right, then the environment 'success factor' multiplies ten-fold because each group is setting incredible standards. I have always seen this as a 'teams-within-a-team' scenario.

I am sure you will enjoy reading this book, as it provides a fascinating insight into a diverse range of world-class, high-performing teams. However, what really stands out are the defining principles common to all. Whether it is sport or business, understanding those principles and having the knowledge to evaluate both people and the environment will help drive people who are good to create their best operating environment.

This book, like great teams, has clarity and shared knowledge – there are many 'pearls'. Reading it, you will feel it is possible to be part of a world-class environment because it gives you the opportunity to understand those key components and what to look for.

The feeling you get from being part of a team delivering unbelievable performances cannot be bettered. There evolves a collective appreciation and trust between everyone involved. It is that feeling which you will never forget.

Enjoy *Stronger Together*. I hope you are in, or have the opportunity to be part of, a great team.

Sir Ian McGeechan OBE

Introduction

The date: 6 April 2014

The venue: Sher-e-Bangla National Stadium, Mirpur, Bangladesh

As a little white cricket ball flies through the air and over the boundary, the Sri Lankan team race onto the field to celebrate. They have won the final of the ICC Twenty20 World Cup. Against all expectations, they are the cricket world champions. Coming into the tournament, Sri Lanka were the fourth favourites. In the final they beat the overwhelming favourites, India, with 15 balls to spare.[1]

The Sri Lankans did not have the best squad of players in the world. They were not the most talented in the competition and they certainly were not the pundits' or bookies' favourites, so how did this team defy expectations? What did they have that enabled them to become the world champions?

The date: 5 May 1980

The location: the Iranian Embassy in London

Two units of Special Air Service (SAS) commandos secured the Iranian Embassy following a five-day terrorist siege. The mission, codenamed Operation Nimrod, aimed to take control of the embassy and rescue the 19 hostages held therein. In just 17 minutes a team of 30 elite SAS soldiers had entered the building, neutralised the terrorist threat and liberated the hostages.

How did they successfully coordinate two units of soldiers in a hostile environment filled with gunfire, smoke, dust, noise and armed terrorists? How did they respond to the sudden changes and unforeseen events as they unfolded? What enabled this team to rescue all the hostages and neutralise the enemy threat without losing any of their own members?

The date: 25 September 2013
The location: San Francisco
Sailing team, Oracle Team USA, complete perhaps the most epic comeback in sporting history to win the 34th America's Cup. After trailing 8–1 to Emirates Team New Zealand on 18 September, they clinched the final winner-takes-all race by 33 seconds and won the series 9–8.

How did this team turn around their performance so dramatically? What did they do to reverse an 8–1 deficit and win the series? How did their leadership pull the team back from the brink of failure and inspire them to victory?

The importance of a great team

Former SAS major Floyd Woodrow once told me, 'I'll never succeed without a team.' Interestingly, he wasn't just referring to his time in the Special Forces or in the British Army. Floyd Woodrow understands that teamwork is vital in all areas of life. I've also come to realise the power of this very simple notion. It's rare that we do anything in isolation. Even when we do things that appear to be solo efforts, we often rely on a team. I recently embarked upon an extreme physical endurance event for charity. Although I ran and cycled on my own, I quickly learned that I needed a great team of people around me. Whatever we are doing, I suspect that our success tends to hinge on the performance of our team. In life, we are often faced with uncertainty and encounter unforeseen challenges. It is during these times that great teams become incredibly valuable.

> 'I don't know what questions we will be asked but I
> know that together, we'll find the answers'
> Floyd Woodrow

Many organisations understand the importance of having good people. In business, teamwork is no longer considered to be 'nice-to-have' but is seen as an essential part of both survival and success.[2] But how many leaders are actually able to turn a collection of good individuals into a great team? How many teams actually become more than the sum of their parts? Having good people does not, in itself, mean that the team will be successful. Daft as it sounds, many organisations do exactly that: pull together some good people, set them to work on a task and then sit back and expect success.

Let's imagine for a moment that the Sri Lankan cricket team adopted that approach. Let's imagine that the best 11 Sri Lankan players arrived at the team hotel, boarded the team bus, drove to the stadium, changed into their identical team kit and then took to the field – as individuals. How likely are they to be crowned world champions?

What is likely to happen if 30 highly trained SAS commandos all meet up at the Iranian Embassy in battle dress with their weapons and equipment, and decide to storm the building? Despite the fact that they're all elite soldiers, I suspect it might be carnage.

I often ask sports teams if they really are a team, or if they just wear the same shirts. Equally, I have asked senior leadership teams and boards of directors if they are genuinely a team or merely a collection of job titles sharing a boardroom. Just because a group of people share the word 'director' in their job title, it does not necessarily make them a team. I'd also argue that simply sharing a brand, or sharing resources, is not enough either.

When I see teams at work, I see people working together. They are collectively invested in a goal and engaged in achieving it. It sounds blindingly obvious, I know, but there are so many collections of people that are called a team but who operate as loosely connected individuals. Rather than working together, they work alongside each other. Anecdotally, many of us know that when a team works well, it can be incredibly powerful. Most leaders and managers realise that high-performing teams give greater results than high-performing individuals who operate independently. There is empirical evidence that reinforces this simple notion. The National Transportation Safety Board found that 78 per cent of the incidents reported in commercial aviation occurred with teams flying together for the first time. NASA also discovered that fatigued crews with a history of working together make half as many errors as crews who are rested but have not worked together before.[3] Clearly, a great team can provide any organisation with a distinct competitive advantage.

What is the essence of a great team?

How, then, do we create highly effective teams? What is it that differentiates the very best teams in the world? Why is it that some teams always seem able to outperform their competition? What do they have that the others don't? What do they do that the others won't? These are the questions that occupy my mind. They spark my curiosity, they constantly agitate my brain cells, and they drive me to find answers.

Why is it that some teams seem to have a telepathic

understanding of each other? Their actions appear to be seamlessly blended, like a flock of starlings or a shoal of herring moving together as one. How are teams able to do this? What can leaders do to develop teams that are capable of this mesmerising synchronicity? How is it that they are able to communicate with a fleeting glance, a wink or a nod of the head? What's the secret to their incredible, almost mystical, level of understanding? Equally, some teams appear to have superstrong bonds. In some cases, their members are literally willing to put their lives on the line for each other. How do leaders develop this intense loyalty within their teams?

Is luck the key?

It is tempting to think that the world's great teams form by chance. Perhaps they just appear when we bring together a collection of high-performing individuals. Maybe it's because they were forged in adversity. Perhaps circumstance forced them to galvanise and become a great team. Or could it be that they just click for some unknown reason?

Of course, the characteristics of world-class teams don't develop by chance. They are not the result of luck or circumstance. If we don't understand the mechanics behind their creation, we might conclude that it 'just happened'. However, the truth is that the greatest teams on earth develop these characteristics over time. They understand how to deliver consistent high performance. There is a mechanism and a rationale.

To understand the secret of their success we need to ask:

- What is their formula?

- What are the common characteristics that world-class teams, from vastly different disciplines, all display?

- How do they recruit and select their team?

- What makes someone a great team player?

- How would we spot one?

- What do they look like and sound like?

- What are the secrets of world-class teamwork?

- How do the greatest teams in the world operate?

- What are the dynamics within the team?

- How do they communicate?

- How do they develop 'togetherness'?

- What allows them to collectively respond to changes in their environment and therefore thrive in chaos?

- How do they build an exceptional culture?

- How do great teams turn around performances when things are going wrong?

- How do they consistently raise the bar and stay ahead of their competition?

- What are the characteristics of world-class leaders?

- What do they do to create teams that are capable of consistently delivering world-class performance?

Let's learn from the best

To answer the questions above, I set out on a mission to study some of greatest teams and leaders on the planet. My rationale is pretty simple. I deliberately sought a selection of teams that are in vastly different disciplines. In many cases, these teams are also subject to extreme demands. If there are characteristics that are shared by elite sports teams, an aerobatic display team, a Formula One pit crew, racing yacht crews and Special Forces units, those characteristics are likely to be pretty generic to all teams. However, it doesn't stop there. What about the greatest animal teams? Would we see the same characteristics in pods of orca and dolphins? Are there lessons that we can learn from these highly successful teams too?

Throughout this book, I'll share what I have found from studying and working with these phenomenal teams. More importantly, we will look at how you can apply these valuable lessons and improve the performance of your teams. Here is a brief introduction to some of the organisations that we will learn from, to give you a flavour.

The Red Arrows

The Red Arrows are the Royal Air Force aerobatic display team. They are widely regarded as the best in the world.[4] Since the team was established in 1964, they have flown over 4,500 displays in 55 countries across the globe. Their motto is *Éclat*, which is French for 'Brilliance'. It is very apt. During displays, the team of nine display pilots can fly at close to 600mph and are often just six feet apart.

SAS units

The Special Air Service (SAS) are an elite special-forces unit of the British Army. Being the first of its kind, the SAS has become the blueprint for other Special Forces regiments throughout the world. Over 50 years after it was established, the SAS is still widely regarded as the best in the world.[5] Although the vast majority of SAS operations are not publicised, the regiment gained worldwide fame and recognition after successfully ending the siege in the Iranian Embassy in London and rescuing all the hostages.[6]

Lotus Formula One pit crew

Formula One pit crews have an extremely demanding job. In the heat, humidity, dust and noise of a Grand Prix race, the crew aim to change all four wheels on the car in approximately 2.5 seconds. Coordinating a team of 23 people to deliver a performance is no easy task. Interestingly, being a member of the pit crew is not a full-time job. In Formula One, members of the pit crew are simply the race engineers, who have a day job ahead of their role in the pit crew. As the race team manager, Paul Seaby, said to me, 'In competition they don't get a warm-up. If they were playing soccer, these guys would have to score a penalty with their first kick of the match.'

Racing yacht crews – America's Cup, Extreme 40s and Clipper Round the World Yacht Race

Racing yacht crews are subject to a number of extraordinary demands that require them to be a great team. During competition they need to collectively respond to changes in the wind, tides, current and race conditions, to name but a few. The Extreme 40s series brings together some of the very best sailors in the world in 14 crews of 5, for an 8-race series, in some of the fastest yachts ever built. The America's Cup competition pitches two of the world's leading yacht clubs against each other for 17 rounds of racing. Crews of 11 compete at speeds of around 35mph in purpose-built boats, for the coveted Auld Mug trophy. It is a very high-speed, highly volatile and incredibly competitive environment. Demanding as these forms of racing are, the amateur crews on the Clipper Round the World Yacht Races have the addition of extreme weather and sea conditions to contend with, as well as the challenge of being crammed together on a boat for up to ten months.

The ISS crew

The International Space Station (ISS) is home to a crew of three astronauts from the North American Space Agency (NASA) and the European Space Agency (ESA), plus three Russian cosmonauts. The crews live for approximately six months in a space little bigger than a typical three-bedroomed house, 240 miles above the earth, travelling at 17,500kmph through the vacuum of space. The crew is incredibly vulnerable and members can find themselves in life-threatening situations at a moment's notice. Of course, if the team isn't working, there is no option to simply walk out and slam the door behind you. These teams cannot swap personnel if things don't work out. The ISS crew is a team that has to work.

Sri Lanka Cricket Team – ICC Twenty20 (T20) World Champions in 2014

For those not familiar with the tournament, the best international cricket teams in the world battle it out to see who can score the most runs with their 120 balls and 11 batsmen. It is the shortest competitive form of cricket, meaning that the momentum shifts can be extremely pronounced. In T20 cricket, the game can change in a handful of deliveries; matches can be decided by a single run. The margin for error is tiny, so every delivery and every run is valuable. Therefore, T20 cricket also requires an extreme level of teamwork between batting partnerships, fielding teams and bowlers.

FIFA World Cup Final officiating team

Soccer referee Howard Webb and his team are unique. As a trio, they are the only team to have officiated in two FIFA World Cup Final tournaments. In addition to appearing in Brazil 2014, Howard's team also took charge of the 2010 FIFA World Cup

Final between Spain and The Netherlands, in South Africa. Although refereeing a soccer match might look like a solo effort, that perception couldn't be further from the truth.

The Boxer Rebellion

The Boxer Rebellion are no ordinary rock band. As well as writing and performing music, the quartet also has its own record label. They have released four highly acclaimed albums, and tour Europe and the world playing to thousands of fans.

Animal teams

In addition to world-class human teams, there are some incredible teams in the animal kingdom. To learn more about how they operate, I spent time with biologist Dr Dan Franks from the University of York. He helped me to understand how pods of orca and schools of dolphins hunt together. You may have seen footage from natural-history documentaries, showing orca in Antarctica washing Weddell seals off ice floes, bottlenose dolphins in Florida trapping fish in a rings of silt and then catching them as they jump to escape, or hunting groups of orca in the North Atlantic catching herring by corralling them in a net of bubbles. Studying teams of animals helps us to understand the fundamental principles by which creatures, including humans, coordinate. Animal teams show us the base principles of teamwork in action with incredible clarity.

Look at your team

As you read this book, you'll naturally begin to reflect on how this applies to your own team. To help, it is often wise to stop and think about your own team from a few different perspectives. Who is 'your team'? It might seem a rather daft question, and one that doesn't need much thought, but bear with me. The business that I work in has two employees: myself and my wife, Caroline. At first glance, it seems that our team is pretty small. However, I look at it very differently. My loose definition of 'our team' includes all the individuals or organisations that have an impact on our success. When I take this perspective, I begin to see that our team includes our suppliers, our customers, advisors and a number of other key partners. We often 'team up' with partners to deliver events or projects. Even a seemingly individual project, such as writing this book, involves a team. Therefore, our team extends way beyond the two of us in the office.

When I posited this idea with a corporate client, they began to realise that the 'hierarchical teams' that they traditionally saw within the organisation were not necessarily the same as the teams that delivered results. Like many businesses, they viewed teams through lines of reporting and management. Their organisational structure shows teams, such as the marketing team or the finance team, reporting to managers. However, in order to deliver results, people often worked with other members of the business outside their departmental team. When we began to view teams as the collections of individuals who work together to deliver results, their perspective changed.

I also notice that teams tend to have many layers and subteams within them. England's World Cup-winning rugby coach, Sir Clive Woodward, noted that the England Rugby Team extended beyond the 15 players that would run out onto the field on match day.[7] In addition to the starting 15, there is an extended squad of players, plus the coaching staff and support teams. Each of these is a team in its own right, as well as being part of the wider team. However, it doesn't stop there. To ensure that England rugby is successful, the coaching and playing team need support from their governing body (the Rugby Football Union), as well as their partners and sponsors. On a smaller scale, there are many teams within the team. There is a leadership team, as well as units on the field such as the back three, the tight five, the front row, the back row and the half-backs. Equally, within the support team there are management and logistics people, sports medics and sports science staff. These are all defined units within the coaching and support team.

With this understanding, I suspect it might be wise to take time and reflect upon your team from several different angles:

- Who is in your team?

- Who has an influence over your success?

- Where are the different sub-teams?

- How many layers are there to your team?

- Who needs to work together to deliver your results?

What can you learn?

In this book I would like to share what I have learned from these extraordinary teams. Although I think it's very beneficial to understand what makes them great, and the characteristics they display, I believe that there is something even more valuable that we can learn. Unlike many other books on teamwork and leadership, I don't want to simply describe world-class teams. I also want to know *how* they became great. How did they develop? What did they do to progress from good to great, and from great to world class? I would argue that these insights will be more valuable to leaders. For example, many people will know that the All Blacks rugby team have a world-class culture. In his book, *Legacy*, James Kerr describes the culture that the All Blacks have created and also explains how they develop it.[8] I believe that this is far more valuable, because it helps us to understand how we can build a great culture using the same principles that the All Blacks adopt.

At the end of each chapter, there is a summary followed by a workshop section. Here you will find key questions that will help you to apply the principles that underpin world-class teams, and by using them you will be able to improve the performance of your own team. In these workshop sections, I also invite you to assess your team against some key characteristics. I'll ask how you would score your team using a simple 0–10 scale, where ten equals 'perfect, flawless and cannot be improved' and zero equals 'there's nothing good about it'. Once you have a score, I would also ask how you could improve this score by just one point. For example, from a 6/10 to a 7/10. There is a sound reason why I suggest looking for just one point improvement, rather than asking how you could get to 10/10 (and it's not a lack of ambition). A one-point improvement is a tangible step.

- How does a 7/10 differ from a 6/10?

- How will we know when we get to a 7/10?

- What will we see and hear that's different when we're a 7/10?

- What do we need to do differently to become a 7/10?

If I were to ask you how you could get to 10/10, I'd be asking how you create perfection, which is arguably an impossible task. Of course, when you become a 7/10, you can ask the same questions to become an 8/10 and so on. In doing so, you can become ever better. This very simple thought powers many performers to become world class.

Many people will read over these questions without really taking time to find the answers or to work out how to implement them. If you finish reading this book and describe it as 'interesting' or 'enjoyable', I think you will have missed a trick. In Chapter 8 we will revisit the workshops, go into more detail, and apply all the information you have learned from the book. I include additional questions to help you build on your knowledge and move forward. Feel free to return to Chapter 8 again and again as you and your team develop, progress and hone your skills further.

If you take time to reflect on how you can use this information, you might describe it as 'transformational'.

CHAPTER 1

World-class Teams

Over the years I have seen some truly world-class teams at work. Some of the sports teams are world champions and European champions. Others have won back-to-back championships in their domestic club competitions. Many of the non-sports teams, such as the Red Arrows and SAS, are recognised as the world leaders in their field. However, these are not the only teams that I've studied and worked with. As well as world-class teams I have also seen some that are very good, others that were good, some that were pretty average, a few that were downright poor and even one or two that were completely abysmal. I learned an enormous amount about teamwork, leadership and culture when I worked in an English Premier League football team that finished bottom of the league and was relegated. Working at that club was not a pleasant experience – the culture stank. However, it was incredibly educational. This diverse experience has given me an interesting perspective and allowed me to compare the differences that exist between teams that are average and those that are good, between good and very good, and between very good and world class. It helps me to identify the subtle differences that separate those true world leaders. Importantly, it also helps to illustrate the ways in which teams can climb the ladder from poor to average, average to good and so on.

The common characteristics of world-class teams

It's hard not to ask yourself what characterises the greatest teams and differentiates them from their competitors. What do they have? Are there common habits and characteristics that exist in great teams that operate in very diverse disciplines? If so, what are they?

Through my studies I have discovered a number of common characteristics that world-class teams exhibit. Initially, I noted five characteristics, but more recently I have added a sixth. My six are not a definitive or exhaustive list, and they will differ slightly from those of other authors who have researched and written about great teams. However, I would challenge you to look at the very best teams on earth and to sense-check these. Do you see these six characteristics in great teams? Teams that are:

1 Highly focused,
   have

2 Shared standards and expectations
   and a

3 Total appreciation of each individual
   that

4 Draw strength from their differences,
   are

5 Brutally honest
   and

6 Always learning

Of course, this is just a list of six headlines. To understand what world-class teams actually do we need to get beyond the headlines. We need to get under the skin of these teams and find out exactly what they do to exhibit these characteristics and how they do it. Let's look at those 'headlines' in detail.

1 Highly focused

This is the foundation upon which all the other elements of a successful team are built. Very simply, world-class teams have a strong, clear and shared purpose. Are you thinking, *That sounds obvious ... there's nothing new or revolutionary here*? Well, I would agree wholeheartedly. Interestingly, I did not say 'common goal'. There is a significant difference between a common goal and a strong, clear, shared purpose. A goal is a statement of what we desire. A purpose is a reason for being. Although team members may have a common goal, it does not mean that they understand their purpose with strength and clarity. I'd argue that most sports teams set out to win. That's their *common goal*, but it doesn't explore their *reason*.

However obvious it might sound, there are very few teams that actually have these three fundamental elements: strong, clear and shared purpose. Each of these is critically important. The purpose must be strong. There has to be a very good reason why each of the members will invest themselves in the team. What are we here to do? What does it mean? Why is it important? Why does it matter? What would happen if we didn't do it?

Identify your strong, compelling purpose

I'm sure that you've heard various people explaining the importance of having a 'compelling reason' or 'a cause', before now. If a team is to become world class, the members have got to have an incredibly strong reason to push themselves, and each other, to excel. It can't be a 'so what?' reason. In Olympic sports you'd imagine that this compelling reason would be obvious. We're here to win an Olympic gold medal, right? That's true, but on its own it's not enough. Successful Olympic athletes often have a fairly extensive and dedicated support team. Even an individual athlete, such as a swimmer or a runner, will have a team that includes their coaches, sport scientists, physiotherapists, strength-and-conditioning specialist, nutritionist and sport psychologist. None of these people will be awarded an Olympic medal if the athlete is successful, so why should the members of the support team push themselves, and each other, to help the athlete to win a medal? If we look at it in the cold light of day, the medal is just a metal disc on a ribbon. What's so special about that? Will it change the world?

In itself, the gold medal is not necessarily compelling. The strength of purpose comes through understanding what Olympic success means to everyone. What's the 'why?'. The meaning goes beyond acquiring a metal disc on a ribbon. An Olympic medal is a mark of success. Contributing to Olympic success gives every-one in the team a way of pushing themselves and exploring their potential, not just the athlete. Enabling the athlete to achieve their potential often requires the support team to do the same. As a sport psychology coach, I'm also pushing to achieve my potential – professionally and intellectually. There will only be one medal presented, and it will be awarded to the athlete. However, when the support team all share this purpose, we begin to realise that the medal provides every one of us with our own Olympic success.

Author Simon Sinek suggests that understanding the 'why?' is central to engaging people.[1] What's the cause and why should I fight for it? Human decision-making is often made on an emo-tional, rather than a rational basis. The cause engages us emotionally. In writing *How To Shine*, I discovered that world-class performers are often powered by passion. This gives them the reason to push themselves through discomfort, overcome all the hurdles and setbacks, and keep going when everyone else has given up. It's no different in a team.

Major Chris Hunter is a leader in the British Army. His specialism is bomb disposal. To many people, the prospect of walking towards a live bomb would seem pretty outrageous. However, Major Hunter explains that the reason is very simple. He and his team have the opportunity to prevent carnage. They have the capability to neutralise a weapon designed to kill and maim large numbers of people. Their compelling reason is pretty obvious: they save lives. For many teams, however, the purpose might not be quite so stark.

World Cup-winning cricket coach, Paul Farbrace, explained that the Sri Lankan cricket team's success was fuelled by emotion and meaning. They had a reason. In the lead up to the tournament, two of Sri Lanka's most respected and loved senior players, Kumar Sangakkara (Sanga) and Mahela Jayawardene, announced that this would be their last T20 World Cup. As Paul Farbrace describes it: 'This was for Sanga and Mahela. Before the final, we prepared a short video with the two of them winning together. It was a real tribute to them and their careers. It was incredibly emotional. There were tears in the room and a lot of people were speechless. We all knew why this was important.'

I would argue that all teams have opportunities to find compelling reasons and to discover the meaning that underpins what they do. As the Sri Lankan cricket team will testify, circumstance can present these opportunities. However, in many cases the deeper 'why?' is part of their inherent reason for being. Some teams make the most of these opportunities and emphasise this meaning. Others fail to grasp the value or importance of it.

Recognise your compelling reason

What is the reason that you do what you do? Go beyond the headlines, beyond 'the what?' and 'the how?'.

If your team made washers (those small black rubber discs that are used in plumbing), what would your compelling reason be? Just to make washers? To make washers so that your company made profit and everyone can pay their bills? To give the shareholders another holiday each year? Is that compelling? If the company wasn't there, people would earn their living elsewhere, so why is it important that this business makes washers? Why should anyone give him or herself to this cause? Often it helps to ask, 'Why is it important to do it well?'

How about if the reason to produce washers was to make household appliances safe and reliable? What if it was to ensure that people could sleep soundly, knowing that they were not going to wake up to a flooded kitchen? What if it was to give families peace of mind, by making the very best and most reliable washers possible?

Simon Sinek explains how Apple differentiates itself from other computer manufacturers. The company doesn't tell the world that it makes great computers that are beautifully designed and user-friendly (that's their 'what?' and 'how?'). Instead, it is an organisation that thinks differently, that challenges the status quo and gives you a new experience.[2] Apple's founder, Steve Jobs, described it as 'making a dent in the universe'.[3] Oh, and they happen to make computers.

Make your purpose clear

World-class teams also have a very clear purpose. They understand their 'what?'. Again, this sounds blindingly obvious, I know. But how many mission statements have you ever seen that are simple and clear? I've seen my fair share of mission statements. Most leave me perplexed as to the organisation's job. Amazingly, researchers at Harvard University discovered that less than 10 per cent of senior executives agreed on the job of their team.[4]

How many teams actually understand their job in the simplest possible terms? In sport, it's often relatively easy to simplify and clarify the task of the athlete and their support team. For several years I worked with a swimmer. He swam the 100m breaststroke. His job, very simply, was to swim two lengths of the pool as quickly as he could. The support team and coaches therefore knew that their job was to help the athlete swim two lengths of a pool as fast as possible.[5] Ben Hunt-Davis describes how Team GB Olympic rowing crews were driven by the question, 'Does it make the boat go faster?'[6] This same question helped power Brendan Hall's boat *Spirit of Australia* to victory in the 2010 Clipper Round the World Yacht Race.[7] It is a very simple question that focuses the minds of the entire team. This level of clarity isn't limited to athletes or even sports. The SAS units involved in the siege at the Iranian Embassy also had a very clear purpose: to rescue the hostages in the building.[8] Even global organisations can clarify their purpose. Fred Smith famously describes the job of FedEx as 'delivering a package overnight'.[9]

Share your purpose

A strong and clear purpose is powerful but, in a team environment, it also needs to be shared. Moreover, it needs to be understood in the same way by each member of the team. When team members genuinely share the purpose of the team, personal agendas and collective agendas become aligned. There is a word that I often hear from teams, which tends not to feature in world-class teams. That word is 'sacrifice'. You may have heard leaders explaining the importance of sacrificing yourself for the team. There is no 'I' in team, right? If there is a misalignment between what is good for me and what's good for the team, then I am forced to choose. In that situation, I may need to sacrifice my own interests for that of the team. But what if my own interests and those of the team were aligned; if those things that were good for the team were also good for me? What if there was no competition between the two? What if I could simultaneously act in my own interests and those of the team? If that were the case, there would be no sacrifice to make. In world-class teams, personal agendas don't seem to compete. In fact, Khoi Tu noticed that great teams serve the interests of their members.[10] Often this happens when the team provides the members with a way of achieving their ambitions. By giving to the team, the members gain. Nowhere is this more obvious than in teams where the members utterly depend on the unit for survival. In some teams, such as pods of orca and SAS units, team performance can literally make the difference between life and death.

2 Share standards and expectations

As well as a shared purpose, the very best teams also have an acute understanding of the standards that they expect from each other. Fundamentally, they know what 'good enough' looks like and they understand it in the same way. Brendan Hall, winning skipper of the Clipper Round the World Yacht Race, said their crew needed to be 'very clear about how hard we want to push – it's not just enough to say "we want to win"'.[11] This simple comment provides a real insight into how his team developed shared standards and expectations. They needed to know what 'pushing hard enough' really meant. What does it look like, sound like and feel like? How would they know when their crew-mates were pushing hard enough? Of course, every team in the race wants to win, but they will all have different ideas as to what constitutes 'pushing hard enough'.

Some human beings will always opt to work at the lowest threshold. Rather than looking to push themselves as far as possible, they'll tend to do as little as possible to get by. You can probably recall some people and environments where you've seen this phenomenon at work. My most striking experience came when I worked in the Premiership football club that I mentioned earlier – the one that finished rock bottom of the league. I saw a pattern starting to develop in the players. If one of them eased off slightly, many of the others would notice and follow suit. I suspect that the conversation between their ears went something like this: 'Hang on, why am I busting my backside if they're taking it easy? Why should I be the only one working hard around here?'

The result is that the trend perpetuates and everyone's standards begin to drop. Each of the players notices those around them easing off. Not wanting to be the only one working hard, they ease off too. As a consequence, the performance of the team plummets.

When we're operating in teams, we have a natural tendency to assess how our fellow teammates are performing. Are they running as hard as I am? Is everyone else putting in the effort too? Do they care as much as I do? Of course, this tendency can also work in our favour. Double-gold-medal-winning Olympic rower Steve Williams described the 'blind trust' that developed within his crews. Everyone in the team knew that the other members were giving all they could. Nobody wanted to be the one to let the side down. It meant that, on Christmas Day, they would all put in a hard training session at home. Steve describes getting on the ergo (rowing machine) in his back garden after he'd eaten his Christmas lunch. Even though the snow lay thick on the ground, Steve (dressed in his woolly hat and gloves) went out and trained hard because he knew that his three teammates would all be doing the same. The primary motive for this rather bizarre behaviour was simple: Steve didn't want to be the one who let the team down.

Here's an example from another English Premier League football team, to help illustrate the point.

How performance can imperceptibly decrease

We'd reached October, having started the season well, but then lost our way. During the first few games we'd won and drawn the majority of matches and were doing well. However, wins had turned to draws and draws to losses. The manager sat down with the coaches one morning before training and said, 'I can't understand it, we're not doing anything differently.' By chance, we'd videoed a training session in the pre-season, a couple of months earlier, so I suggested that we also video the session that morning and compare the two. Later that day we watched the two sets of footage side-by-side.

Far from 'not doing anything differently', we witnessed two vastly different sessions. Although the drills were the same, the way the players applied themselves was not. The intensity and pace, the accuracy and precision, the sharpness and competitiveness were all distinctly better in our pre-season session a couple of months earlier. However, the coaches had not noticed the standards dropping over the weeks. In reality, they didn't fall in one go. Instead, the players had eroded the standards by an almost invisibly small amount each session – just a fraction of a per cent. We'd seen the effect of this on the score sheet before noticing it on the training field.

When I reflect back on that experience, I suspect that I did notice the slide but didn't say anything. It almost felt petty. Pulling the players up and saying, 'That's not good enough' seemed a little anal, because the drop in standards was so small. I remember thinking, *I'm sure it's just a tiny blip and it'll be better tomorrow*. But every time we accept a 'blip' we reset the bar to a lower point. In reality, my decision to remain silent dictated that the lower standard was acceptable. To enforce the standards, we need a clear idea as to what 'good enough' looks like, sounds like and acts like. Twice-Michelin-starred chef Kenny Atkinson once told me that he tastes the food with his chefs so that they have a shared understanding of what constitutes under-seasoned, over-seasoned and properly seasoned. He doesn't rely on each chef's own opinion as to whether it tastes 'right' or 'nice'.

Do you and your team know what 'good enough' looks like, and do you understand it in the same way? Would you recognise if the standard slipped by a fraction of a per cent, and what would you do about it? Can you recognise if the standards are eroding before you see the effect on the scoreboard?

3 Total appreciation of each individual

There are often many distinct and diverse roles within a team. Often there is a hierarchy that seems to develop. Some of these roles are seen as more important than others. The natural extension is that we might start to perceive that some people are more important than others. If this separation begins to appear, it's also possible that we will struggle to see the value that each individual brings to the team. In contrast, the very best teams in the world seem to have an acute appreciation of each individual and the contribution they make. In many cases, they understand that the team could not function without all the members. Imagine a rock band on stage without their drummer or bass guitarist. Although these members of the team might not be at the front of the stage in the spotlight, the rest of the band know that they cannot play without the rhythm and the beat that comes from their teammates in the background. Great teams know that the machine doesn't function unless all the cogs turn together – however big or small they might be.

I often ask a question when working with teams: 'How valued and valuable do your people feel?' Although 'valued' and 'valuable' sound similar, there is a profound difference between feeling valued and feeling valuable. If the people around me give me lots of positive feedback, which tells me how grateful they are, I am likely to feel valued. However, I may not feel valuable. If I intrinsically understand the contribution that I make, and the positive impact I have, I am likely to feel valuable. I often see teams of volunteers at work, such as a school fundraising committee. My wife will often stay up well past midnight, baking cakes for the school bake sale, because she knows that the others are relying on her to do her bit. When there are only a few core members of the team, everyone realises that the team is dependent upon them and that their input is crucial. It also tends to be very motivating to know that you're important. Many people will go to incredible lengths when they know others are relying on them.

How does this apply to you?

The chief executive of a large charity approached me and asked if I could deliver a motivational keynote at the charity's annual conference. Very simply, he wanted me to inspire the team. The charity's mission was to help those who were on the fringes of society to get back on their feet – typically those who were homeless or using drugs. That sounded like a pretty inspirational cause to me, so why did the CEO need me? As we chatted, it became apparent that the majority of the 3,000-strong organisation didn't work on the front line. Because they didn't directly work at the sharp end, they didn't realise the importance of their role.

I delivered a very simple session during the conference, which showed those furthest from 'the coal face' how their contribution was vital in helping the vulnerable people the charity served. We literally helped Mary, who did the filing in the office, to understand how vital her contribution was. Mary began to understand that without her, the fundraising team couldn't do their job well. If the fundraising team didn't do their bit, the support team could not do their job well. If the support team couldn't deliver, then the front-line team would not be able to help those on the streets who most needed help. This very simple exercise helped Mary, and her colleagues, to understand how valuable their contribution is to the organisation and the vulnerable people whom they serve. They began to realise how their admin role at head office actually helped change people's lives.

Interestingly, the very best leaders that I have seen often go a stage further. They actively ask for input from the team. Chef Kenny Atkinson will often request feedback on new dishes. He doesn't just ask his senior chefs, or indeed the junior chefs. Kenny asks his entire team, including the kitchen porters who do the cleaning and wash the dishes. Often they may not give any feedback at all. When they do offer a suggestion, it could be ridiculous. However, occasionally it is the kitchen porter who provides the real gem. Kenny knows that if you don't ask them for input, you'll never get that gem. Perhaps more importantly, when you do ask for their input you engage them and allow them to understand that they are valued and valuable to the team.

How to create 'alignment': a common purpose

I use a very simple principle with organisations to help each member understand how they can best contribute. The first stage is to understand the job of the organisation in the simplest possible terms, in the same way that Olympic swimmer Chris Cook realised that his job was to swim two lengths of the pool as quickly as he could. What is the 'two lengths of the pool' equivalent for your organisation?

Once we know this, we can start to cascade this question down through the organisation. What is the 'two lengths' for each of the departments or teams within the organisation? How do they contribute to the 'two lengths' of the organisation as a whole? It makes sense that all the teams' 'two lengths' should align and contribute completely to the job of the organisation.

The next stage is to ask exactly the same question of the individuals within those teams. What is their personal 'two lengths'? How does it contribute to that of their team, and therefore the organisation? Again, there should be a clear alignment between each person's role and that of their team. There should also be a clear link between the job of the team and the organisation. When we have this, each person has a clear understanding of where he or she fits and where everyone else fits around them. They are also able to understand how their contributions, and those of their team members, are vital to the success of their team and the entire organisation.

I once heard a story about a man who swept the floors in a hanger at NASA. His job was to help ensure that no dust or debris got into the working parts of the spacecraft. When he was asked what he did at NASA he said, 'I help put rockets in the sky.'

4 Draw strength from their differences

Each of us is as unique as our fingerprints. Even identical twins with the same DNA have a different life experience, different skills, perspectives and personalities that they bring to the world. As a result, every team has an element of diversity. There will always be inherent differences between team members. These differences give the opportunity for strength but also the potential for weakness. In fact, as the amount of difference between people increases, so does the potential for both strength and weakness. Groups of human beings inevitably have different perspectives and opinions.

They also have different values and beliefs. They are likely to have differing solutions to any given problem. These differences can lead to conflict. Therefore, those teams with the greatest diversity have an interesting challenge. Can they manage those differences to gain the greatest strength? Or will those differences lead to cracks that divide the team? How do we ensure that our team is not a collection of misfits but a well-oiled machine?

FIFA World Cup Final referee Howard Webb explained that there was often tension between him and one of his assistant referees. The pair had very different characters and often wildly different perspectives. It meant that they often didn't see eye-to-eye or get on together socially. Although this created challenges, they were an incredibly effective team and had the utmost respect for each other.

Great leaders, and teams, invest time and effort in understanding each member. What are their tendencies? What kind of personality do they have? How do they communicate? What motivates them and 'makes them tick'? How do they respond to tough challenges, pressure, criticism, success, praise, and so on? Great leaders will often ensure that they know the answers to these questions.

How to start understanding

The first step is often to understand a person's personality and how it impacts on the way they communicate and how they are motivated. Psychologist Carl Jung identified a range of personality types that revolve around our tendencies.[12] Since Jung's initial work, other psychologists and researchers have created models, theories and inventories that assess and categorise our personality type. You may have seen the Myers-Briggs Type Indicator (MBTI), the DISC (which stands for Dominance, Inducement, Submission and Compliance) or Insights Discovery profiles. Each has a slightly different way of depicting and explaining differences in personality. They recognise that we all have some characteristics that tend to dominate and others that tend not to. For example:

- Some people tend to be competitive, demanding, determined, strong-willed and purposeful.

- Others might be more sociable, dynamic, energetic, creative, persuasive and instinctive.

- There are people who tend to be more caring, patient, nurturing and harmonising.

- And there are others who are precise, methodical, structured, conservative, deliberate and reasoned.

Some people have an informal style of communicating; they're the ones who might add a kiss at the bottom of an email. Others are very dry, formal, functional and to-the-point. There is a chance that one person might take offence if they receive an email with no warmth. However, there is a good chance that the person sending it is simply communicating information with no frills. Equally, others might get frustrated when they receive emails that they perceive are full of irrelevant fluff.

Different personalities also vary in the amount of risk they are willing to take and the speed at which they make decisions. These differences often come to the surface in strategic teams.

How does this apply to you?

I have seen tension in the boardroom between those members who tend towards fast-paced, high-risk decisions and the more conservative members that work to a slower pace and are more risk averse. In some cases, leaders can fail to gain the greatest value from the diversity because they don't manage the conversation within the team. Those who work, and think, at a slower pace sometimes do so because they think in more depth. They'll often approach a challenge from a number of different angles and analyse in more detail. It is common for fast-paced leaders to agree actions and move the discussion on to the next subject while the thinkers are still thinking. The greatest leaders often recognise this and deliberately pause to collect the input from everyone, before making decisions and moving on. This way, the team gains the benefit of the deeper thinking that is done by the thinkers.

Great teams often have a balance of these attributes, and know how to integrate them. They appreciate the importance and contribution of all these characteristics and their value to the team. Conversely, in many teams conflict arises when two very different personalities, who value different things, clash.

Managing the diversity

Several years ago I worked with a café restaurant business. Our executive chef was a flamboyant character. He was very unstructured, spontaneous and creative – and he produced delicious food. Our finance director (FD) was very organised, structured, methodical and precise – and was great with the finances. One day the FD asked the chef, 'How many grams of salt do you put in this dish?' The chef replied, 'Until it tastes right.' This answer was not what the FD had hoped for. He asked again and got the same response.

Left to their own devices, the FD would have become frustrated with the chef and conclude that he's unreasonable and that he is being deliberately uncooperative. The head chef would think the FD is just a bean counter who doesn't understand cooking – so what's the solution? They are both brilliant individuals but they're not working together.

▶

The FD explained why he needed a number. 'I have a spreadsheet with a cell and I need to put a number in the cell. We are going to make thousands of these dishes across many restaurants in the next year. I need to know how much salt in each dish, so that I can calculate the cost of salt through the year, the amount of storage we'll need and so on.'

The chef explained that the ingredients are never exactly the same; they come from different suppliers and are grown in different soil at different times of the year, meaning that the natural salt content within the ingredients varies. Sometimes the ingredients contain less salt, so he needs to add slightly more, and vice versa.

To reach a workable solution, we asked the head chef to weigh 50g of salt into a container before he started cooking. When he'd finished we weighed it again to see how much he'd used. Over the course of the month we found that the amount of salt varied between 4.5g and 6g, and averaged 5g. This gave the FD more detail than he'd originally asked for, which gave him additional benefit. The head chef also gained a greater understanding of how to manage his stock levels. It became a win–win rather than a tug of war.

Great leaders and teams manage the diversity to ensure that they draw strength from the differences rather than allowing cracks to appear.

5 Brutally honest

World-class teams have the ability to be completely, and sometimes brutally, honest with each other. They are willing to push themselves and their teammates. They demand more from each other. They ask the really tough questions, and answer them. All these things tend to be uncomfortable. Brutal honesty means having difficult conversations. Often it means departing from harmony and embracing conflict.

I often see honesty being a crucial ingredient in success:

honesty + difference in opinion (which we get from
diversity within the team)
+ genuine value from each individual (which we uncover
when we actively seek their input)
= creative tension

Creative tension is an all-important primer in driving innovation and creativity. It is also vital for those who want to constantly get better. Continuous improvement requires us to look in detail at what we're doing and how we can refine it. Inevitably this exercise requires us to be critical. In a team environment, therefore, we need to be critical of ourselves and each other. However, it doesn't stop there. I've observed how a lack of brutal honesty can weaken a team.

How does this apply in practice?

Recently I was asked to work with a team of business leaders. During the session I explained the six characteristics of world-class teams that I've observed. I asked them to score themselves on their ability to be brutally honest, using a 0–10 scale. There was a wide range of opinions from the group and a heated debate broke out. As the next few minutes unfolded, several members of the group shared what they really felt about the team. I described it as the members of the team beginning to vocalise 'The Great Unsaid'. By this, I simply mean that they were now discussing all those things that they'd been thinking but not saying.

After the session, I chatted to the managing director. He realised that the process was uncomfortable but necessary. Left unsaid, these issues would start to erode the integrity of the team from the inside. We described it like a fallen tree branch in the middle of the forest. Almost as soon as it hits the floor it begins to rot from the inside. When you look at it many weeks later, there is little visible difference. However, when you pick it up and apply a little stress to it, you discover that the strength has been eaten away and the branch crumbles in your hand.

The same is potentially true if The Great Unsaid is allowed to have the same effect on a team. If the core is rotten, the team will also crumble when stress is applied.

Aim for goal harmony

Some will argue that great teams need to be harmonious and that everyone should get along. Although harmony is not in itself negative, an environment without conflict might be limited. Equally, brutally honest teams don't look for a fight, but they don't avoid voicing differences of opinion when they are needed either. Sir David Brailsford is the performance director of British Cycling and Team Sky. He explains that goal harmony is far more important than social harmony in successful teams. In talking about the relationship between Sir Bradley Wiggins and Chris Froome, ahead of the Tour de France, he told BBC Sport: 'I don't spend a nanosecond worrying whether they get on. People talk about having team unity and team harmony. I don't buy that at all. Most of the best teams I've been with, they're not harmonious environments. This is not a harmonious environment. This is a gritty environment where people are pushing really hard. What you need is goal harmony, and there's a big difference between the two.'[13]

How can you develop brutal honesty?

The world-class teams that I've studied have the ability to be very frank with each other in an utterly respectful way. They are happy to give and receive critical feedback. They will have intense discussions and disagreements, and then be able to leave the room and go for a drink together. FIFA World Cup referee Howard Webb said, 'Off the field we'd have some proper arguments – tell each other exactly what we think.' Despite this, he has an incredible level of respect for his fellow referees as people. Their track record shows that they're not only a successful team in the short term, but they also have sustainable working relationships that have spanned many years.

How can world-class teams do this? Importantly, they know that the criticism is not personal. It is not a competition to see who can look best or who can win the argument. The purpose of the conversation is not to flex the ego. The purpose is to help the team deliver its 'two lengths of the pool'. When everyone knows that is the aim of the conversation, it is much easier to engage in critical discussions.

When the team's purpose is strong, clear and shared, they are much more willing to engage in brutally honest discussions. I have often found that there is a gap between what team members think and what they're willing to say. Sometimes they will hold back if they think their comments might hurt someone's feelings, or if they perceive that there could be some retribution. On other occasions, people will not voice their thoughts and feelings if they are continually ignored. It is also common for people to keep their thoughts to themselves if the rest of the group take an opposing viewpoint. How many people are willing to provide that lone dissenting voice? For many people, being 'the odd one out' requires a healthy dose of courage.

I have seen the very best teams actively bucking the sophist notion that the majority must be right. History tells us that the majority can indeed be wrong. In the Middle Ages, for example, it was generally believed that the earth was flat. Therefore, world-class teams deliberately seek out the critical and sceptical voices.

Adam Steltzner led a disparate group of NASA space engineers in a nine-year project to land the one-tonne rover, *Curiosity*, on the surface of Mars using the Sky Crane. He describes their challenge as, 'throwing a dart at a dartboard twenty thousand feet away'. To achieve the mission, his core team was made up of around 40 experts. However, in total there were about 7,000 people involved in the *Curiosity* project. To achieve the mission, Adam Steltzner explains how he created a 'very big table'. He created a very flat, non-hierarchical, structure. He also invited people to cross the boundaries of their intellectual and practical territories, to delve into the boundaries of others, to get cross-pollination of ideas and to get everybody bought into the team's effort. It is an approach that was documented by Norbert Wiener in his book *Cybernetics*.[14] Wiener, a prominent mathematician, developed concepts by inviting a selection of bright people to dinner for lively and unrestrained conversations. In these conversations people ran the gauntlet of acute, good-natured critique and were not allowed to hide behind their perceived expertise. He described the environment by saying, 'It was a perfect catharsis for half-baked ideas, insufficient self-criticism, exaggerated self-confidence, and pomposity. Those who could not stand the gaff did not return, but among the former habitués of these meetings there is more than one of us who feels that they were an important and permanent contribution to our [intellectual] unfolding.'[15]

This approach formed the basis of the brutally honest culture in Adam Steltzner's team, which helped them to successfully land their mobile science laboratory onto the surface of Mars.

Encourage others to take responsibility

What is it that allows great teams to be brutally honest? What stops these very frank discussions from descending into a barrage of finger pointing and blame? Very simply, everyone in the team takes complete responsibility for his or her own performance. By covering their own base first, they're able to offer critical feedback. Without this key ingredient, it is likely that the conversations become a fire fight of accusations.

A couple of years ago I witnessed a head coach lose his cool during a competitive game. The team had been struggling, the crowd were on his back and his job was on the line. During this particular game, the team were losing fairly heavily when one of the officials penalised them for ill discipline. As a consequence, they were marched 15 yards back towards their own end zone. The head coach didn't agree with the call – he had been getting increasingly frustrated by the performance and the fact that they were losing at home. As a result, he lost his cool. The coach tore off his headset, threw it on the ground and marched onto the field screaming at the officials. The result? Another 15-yard penalty.

Now, the combined 30-yard penalty did the team and the coach no favours. However, that wasn't the biggest issue. The problem for the coach is that he couldn't go into the locker room with the team and say, 'You have to be more disciplined than that. You can't keep giving away stupid penalties and costing us 15 yards.' Of course, the players' response is likely to be, 'What about you?' The coach's first job was to say to the players, 'I need to be more disciplined than that. I just cost us 15 yards. I need to be better than that.' Only through doing this could he have really honest discussions with the players.

A great lesson in taking responsibility

I also heard an elite coach talking to two of his players. The two players had missed a pass during the game, which had cost the team dearly. After the game, the coach asked them what had happened with the pass. The passer pointed at the receiver and said, 'He was in the wrong place.' The receiver pointed back to the passer and said, 'He made a bad pass.' The coach then looked at the two of them and said, 'You're both right and you're both wrong. Your pass wasn't accurate and you were in the wrong place. But if you both keep thinking the way you are now, you'll miss the next pass too. The best answer is "I made a bad pass" and "I was in the wrong place". If you accept responsibility for your bit, you'll make the change and connect the pass. If it's always his responsibility, neither of you will change and you'll both keep missing the pass.'

Genius!

6 Always learning

World-class teams have a united desire to be better today than they were yesterday, and better tomorrow than they are today. It is a remarkably simple principle, which drives them to excel. They have an acute awareness that, however good they are right now, they can always improve. Coupled with that is a desire to become the best that they can possibly be. The combination of these ingredients leads them to start asking questions such as, 'How can we improve this area of our game?', 'Where can we tighten up?', 'What can we do to become more consistent?' and 'How can we gain an extra couple of per cent?'

Teams such as the Red Arrows ensure that they employ a very tight 'plan, do and review' cycle. Whereas many teams will review on a monthly, quarterly or annual basis, the Red Arrows review each and every performance on a daily basis. Often they will perform multiple displays in a day. Sometimes they will perform in the same place on consecutive days. It would be easier for them to take the lazy option and conclude that they don't need a thorough review session today because they're performing in the same place tomorrow. They could also decide that they've done really well today, so rather than reviewing for 20 minutes they can afford to finish up earlier. Polar expedition leader Alan Chambers described how his teams always debrief at the end of a day. Sometimes this means spending an extra hour at the end of an exhausting 28-hour trek across a polar ice cap. Most people would excuse them if they decided to call it a day and get to sleep rather than reviewing. However, Alan knows that the debrief is crucial to their success.

How does this apply to you?

Interestingly, many businesses don't review their performance on a daily or even a weekly basis. If polar expedition teams can find time to debrief after 28 hours hauling sleds in sub-zero temperatures, surely business teams could find the time too.

It is these seemingly tiny differences that separate world-class teams from the rest. Regardless of whether the performance was good, bad or average, the very best teams will always ask what they can learn from it and how they can use the experience to get better.

How to take on the world's best – improve faster!

I was asked a simple question by the head coach and performance director of an international sports team who had an interesting challenge: 'How do we beat Australia?' The Aussies were the team's biggest rivals and the number-one team in the world. In recent years the team had experienced little success against the Australians in head-to-head games and couldn't seem to break their dominance. Of course, the Aussies were also getting better all the time and were starting ahead.

The solution that we discussed was fairly simple, but not easy. Our task was to increase the gradient of our progression curve so that it became as steep as possible. The way to do it, very simply, was to intensify the rate at which we learn and improve. We had to learn more and learn faster than we had been doing. In essence, we had to squeeze every possible lesson and gain every ounce of benefit from the experiences that we had. As with many international teams, we didn't have direct contact with the players on a daily basis because they spent most of the time with their clubs. However, we had to use the time we did have with them more intensively and ensure that we made as much progress as we could during that time. We also had to optimise every moment with the coaching and support team. This meant learning the lessons, putting them into practice quickly and making positive changes on the field.

It seems obvious to say that this all requires a high-quality debrief. Having seen hundreds of debrief sessions, and conducted a few, experience tells me that both the frequency and the effectiveness of these sessions can vary markedly from one team to the next. Simply having a review session is not enough to make any team world class. The way in which they are conducted determines the value that the team gains from them. As you'd imagine, the level of brutal honesty that exists within the team will have a significant impact. Former Red Arrows team leader Jas Hawker explained that there is a very simple protocol that helps them to gain value from their post-performance reviews. In the Red Arrows, the team leader kicks off any critical discussions by outlining what they could have done better. The leader then asks the team, 'What do you think I could have done better?' This simple gesture gives the rest of the team the licence and freedom to follow suit. There is a saying in the military: 'You leave your rank at the door in a debrief.'

Summary

We have looked at what differentiates world-class teams. The points I've raised are not the only characteristics of teams. There are many other accounts that describe great teams using different criteria. Having observed many teams at work, I see these six characteristics consistently differentiating those that are world class from those that are very good, in a wide range of diverse disciplines. There are lots of other characteristics that you could see in great teams. You could say, for example, that effective communication is common to great teams. However, I have seen good and even some average teams communicate effectively. Therefore, I don't see characteristics like this as differentiators. Equally, I'm not saying that world-class teams are perfect in these areas. There is always scope to improve. What I have observed is the consistent presence of these characteristics within the world-class teams that I have worked with and studied over the years.

- Be highly focused. Have a strong, clear and shared purpose. Find your compelling reason for what you want to achieve ('Why is important to do it well?'). Identify your clear purpose as a team and then each person's job in the team. Make sure that each member of the team understands the purpose and that it is shared by the team.

- Have shared standards and expectations. Ensure that each team member knows what working towards your goal feels like, looks like or sounds like so that everyone is working to the same ideal. Everyone in the team should know that the other members are giving all they can. To enforce the standard, everyone needs to understand what 'good enough' looks like in the same way.

- Practise total appreciation of each individual. Understand the interdependency between the members. Each person should feel valued and valuable. Seek input from each member of the team, however minor their role might seem to be on the face of it. This will help to avoid missing important information and will also encourage everyone to feel a part of the team and to reinforce its common purpose.

- Draw strength from each person's differences. Manage, and benefit from, the diversity of your team members. Draw strength from the differences rather than allowing cracks to appear. Recognise the varying attributes of your team members and the differences in how people do things. For example, before making decisions, allow time for contributions from those who may take longer than others because their approach is different.

- Be brutally honest. When issues are left unsaid, they will create difficulties that can cause the team to crumble under stress. Aim for goal harmony and encourage others to take personal responsibility – remember, if it's always someone else's responsibility, neither of you will change and you'll both keep missing your goal.

- Always aim to learn and improve. In situations where you are up against great opposition, your team needs to learn to improve faster than in the past and to gain as much benefit as possible from your experiences.

- Take a moment to look at the teams around you. What characteristics do you see in your team? Are there traces of the six characteristics outlined in this chapter? Do you get fleeting glimpses or do you see them consistently and in abundance? Are there certain characteristics that are stronger in your team, and others that need some development?

Throughout the course of this book we will look at how world-class leaders and teams create these characteristics. What do they do that others don't? How can leaders adopt these principles to develop themselves and their teams?

WORKSHOP: The characteristics of world-class teams

How does your team rate against the six characteristics discussed in this chapter? Take a moment and score your team on each of the six, using a simple 0–10 scale. You might find it useful to write it in a notebook. In this scale, a score of 10 means 'perfect, flawless, cannot be improved'. A score of zero means that there is nothing good about it.

1 Highly focused
2 Shared standards and expectations
3 Total appreciation of each individual
4 Draw strength from their differences
5 Brutal honesty
6 Always learning

What can you do to improve your score for each by just one? Use the summary above to help you create a strategy that will work for your team. Guiding people to focus on increasing

▶

the score by just one point is an important coaching principle. When we focus on improving a score of 5 to become a 6, we can create a really tangible and useful strategy. It might also help to ask:

1 What does a 6 look like, and how does it differ from a 5?
2 What will you be doing differently when you're a 6?
3 How will you know when you've become a 6? What will you see and hear?

CHAPTER 2

Recruitment and Selection

Many organisations will talk openly about the importance of having 'the right people'. Some explicitly state that they aim to attract 'the best people'. It makes complete sense that the success of any organisation is heavily influenced by the quality of its people. World Cup-winning rugby coach Sir Clive Woodward says that to create a winning team you need 'the raw materials; the players'.[1] Khoi Tu concluded that great teams, such as the leadership team at Pixar and the Ferrari team that dominated Formula One at the turn of the millennium, are made up of extremely talented individuals.[2] As they construct their team, these organisations deliberately hand-pick the very best individuals in their field. It is an approach that some of the world's wealthiest sports teams use when recruiting. Soccer clubs such as Real Madrid have a track record of paying the biggest money for the biggest stars. But it doesn't always lead to the greatest success. Talent is undoubtedly important, but a collection of talented individuals does not a world-class team make.

Although it might be true that world-class teams seek out the best people, there is a difference between 'a team of superstars' and a 'superstar team'. European Ryder Cup captain Colin Montgomerie stated that he aimed to pick the 'best 12' golfers, not the '12 best'. Although his decision caused a great deal of controversy at the time, it proved to be successful when his team gained the

14½ points required to beat the USA.[3] Colin Montgomerie's views are echoed by FIFA referee Howard Webb. He explained why he was selected to referee the 2010 World Cup Final: 'We weren't the best individuals but we were the best team.'

How, then, do world-class teams recruit members to their organisations? Once they have the members they need, how do they select teams for specific projects or tasks? How are elite squads recruited in sport, and how do coaches select a team for specific games? That's the focus of this chapter.

How does this apply to you?

Do you recruit and select individuals, or do you build a team? Do you recruit people according to their CV and performance in an interview? Do you look at skills, knowledge and experience, or do you assess their character? There is a profound difference between the way that most organisations recruit and select, and the methods employed by the greatest teams and leaders in the world.

Recruitment – what to aim for

The very best organisations know what they're looking for. They know what 'the right person' looks like. There are a number of different levels to this understanding. Is this person a good fit with the culture of our organisation? Do they share our values and our aspirations? Do they reflect the levels of professionalism and the standards that we uphold? Many of the sports teams that I have worked with recognise the importance of recruiting people first and players second. Their first step is often to focus on the qualities that the person brings, before looking at their attributes as a player. It is a philosophy that is also found outside sport.

Twice-Michelin-starred chef Kenny Atkinson recruits chefs to his kitchen team on 'attitude not skills'. In his words, 'We can teach them the skills, but it's hard to teach anyone who has the wrong attitude.' It is a philosophy that is endorsed by the victorious Clipper Round the World Yacht Race skipper, Brendan Hall. He emphasises that, 'I'd rather have a clueless amateur who was willing to learn and is a great team player over a technically gifted and skilful sailor with a negative attitude.'

Elite sports teams often look for 'coach-ability' in players: are they willing to learn and to be coached? Is this person responsible and self-critical about their game? The leading teams will look at how players respond when they're struggling to find their form, or when they're injured. How does the player perform on the big occasions? Do we see the best in them or a shadow of what they're capable of? What happens if they are playing in a team where everyone has their backs against the wall? Do they step forward and take a lead, or do they resort to moaning and blame? These are important considerations when recruiting members to an organisation. Interestingly, Sir Clive Woodward explained that after losing the 1999 Rugby World Cup he was careful to recruit 'energisers' rather than 'energy sappers' into the squad.[4]

Recruiting a Starr

Bart Starr was perhaps the greatest American football quarterback of his generation. He led his Green Bay Packers team, with coach Vince Lombardi, to multiple championship wins and the first two Super Bowl crowns. He was voted the MVP (Most Valuable Player) in the Super Bowl and was also the League MVP in 1966. It might surprise you to know that this undoubtedly world-class player was recruited in the 17th round of the draft as the 199th overall pick.

▶

What made the Packers draft Bart Starr?

Bart Starr was a student at the University of Alabama. Although he played American Football, it was the basketball coach (Johnny Dee) who noticed him and recommended him to the personnel director (Jack Vainisi) at the Packers. Rather than focusing on his skills as a quarter-back, the Packers were convinced that Starr had the ability to succeed in the National Football League (NFL) and would learn quickly.[5] It seems that the Packers recruited Bart Starr because of his ability to learn, and therefore his potential to become great.

How do we know if this person has 'the right attitude'?

In many cases the answer may not be immediately apparent. How do we know what a person will be like when they're struggling or when their team hits a tough patch? One solution might be to ask them. There is a chance that this might provide some useful information. It's likely that the person will tell you what they think you want to hear, or give you their subjective viewpoint, rather than giving an honest objective view. It is also likely that you'll gain greater insight from what they don't say, rather than what they do say. Another solution is to do some background research. This is an approach that the more progressive sporting organisations are now adopting. Often they'll ask other coaches or players that have experience of working with the person they're looking to recruit. Asking some pointed questions to discover how the player responded during a tough season can prove to be very useful. In sports, there might be some evidence such as video footage or other performance data that might also provide an insight. Many of the best organisations will spend a considerable amount of time doing their research before recruiting new members to the team.

Recruiting new members could potentially disrupt a culture. This disruption could be either positive or negative, depending upon the people you add. Therefore it is crucial that organisations know the likely cultural impact that any new additions will have. Can we handle a maverick? Do we need people to shake up the organisation, or not? Should we recruit people with more stability and maturity or those who bring youth and energy? Is a highly talented 'moaner' going to have a positive impact, or not? What impact will this person have?

Challenge your assumptions

Of course, cultural fit is not the only consideration. The person's knowledge, skills and experience are also important. Great teams also tend to be acutely aware of the requirements they have for any role and therefore the person who will be best suited to it. This understanding comes when we're able to identify exactly what characteristics are required to be successful in specific roles.

I recently worked with a business that was heavily focused on telesales. Naturally, a large proportion of the staff were sales people. As you'd imagine, much of their recruitment activity also centred on the sales team. I asked them which members of their team consistently out-performed the rest. It turned out that there were a handful of people who always seemed to exceed targets. I then asked what attributes these people had in common. The answers surprised the leadership team.

Traditionally, they had recruited 'bubbly' people, who were energetic, friendly and easy to get along with. It was always assumed that an out-going personality would be better suited to telesales because they tended to create rapport quickly. However, when they looked at their best performers, they noticed that 'organisation', 'a methodical approach' and 'persistence' actually lead to success. As a result, they have changed what they look for in new recruits and deliberately look for those with a more structured approach.

Who is right for you?

What does the right person look like for your organisation? Obviously, the 'right person' for one organisation will not be the same as for another. Many people's recruitment decisions are based on their intuitive feeling following an interview with a candidate. For experienced interviewers, this method may provide some success. However, often, panels of people are involved. I recently listened to a panel discussing a candidate post-interview. Much of their discussion was informed by their gut-feeling about the person and whether they liked them. No doubt there is some validity to this. However, it might not provide a fully rounded viewpoint. To make the discussion slightly more comprehensive, we drew up a simple set of criteria on which to rate the potential recruit. We asked them to consider, on a scale of 0–10, the recruit's

1   Cultural fit/likeability

2   Coach-ability/willingness to learn

3   Credibility

4   Ability to manage themselves and self-start

5   Willingness to take ownership of issues and find solutions

6   Listening and questioning skills

7   Appetite for a challenge

8   Ability to take responsibility and be self-critical

Of course, these criteria suited this particular organisation. If you were to draw up a set of criteria to use as part of a post-interview debrief, what would *you* include?

How to recruit for a team

Former Red Arrows leader Jas Hawker revealed that the Red Arrows have a rather unique recruitment policy. Unlike many other teams, they recruit three new pilots every year into a team of nine. Each year, one-third of the team members are new recruits. In addition, the Red Arrows replace their three most senior pilots every year. This level of upheaval within the team presents them with a considerable challenge. How do they manage to gel the team in a matter of weeks and become capable of delivering world-class aerobatic displays day after day?

The first step, as Jas explains, is to recruit the best team players. Interestingly, the aim is not to recruit the three best pilots. In Jas's words, 'They're all great pilots. If they weren't great pilots, they wouldn't be there.' Years of experience have given the Red Arrows the understanding that a successful team performance requires the best team players. Their process is fairly simple. The Red Arrows start with 30 candidates for the three positions. From these 30 pilots, 9 are selected to attend a week's training in Cyprus. During the week away, each candidate is interviewed for 20 minutes. In addition there is a flying test, which Jas describes as '20 minutes of pure stress'. The result of the flying test is measured on a simple pass or fail. If you pass, however narrowly, you stay in contention. The rest of the week in Cyprus focuses on assessing how each candidate functions as a team player. The candidates will be presented with a diverse range of challenges, and their responses are observed. How do they respond when criticised? What are they like under pressure? Is their personal agenda really aligned with the team's agenda? Are they here because they want to look good or because they see this as a cosy assignment, or are they here because it massages their ego? The answers to these questions allow the team to gradually whittle the group of potential recruits down to just three. Those who prove to be the best team players will qualify.

In order to recruit 'a great team player' we need to know exactly what one looks like, sounds like and behaves like. In fact, the same principle applies to any other attribute that we identify, so, how can we test for it? What can we do to ensure that our recruits have these qualities?

The Red Arrows know that it comes down to the choices that a person makes. Great team players are:

- Those who choose to take responsibility

- Those who choose to commit to the team

- Those who choose to put the team first

- Those who choose to align to team goals

- Those who choose to accept criticism, be honest, open and admit faults

During the week away, the existing team members are able to see how each recruit responds to different challenges and the choices they make. This information helps them to recruit the best team players.

This simple philosophy underpins the way that America's Cup yacht-racing crews are recruited. Jono MacBeth is a three-time America's Cup winner and was part of the Oracle Team USA crew that won dramatically in 2013. He explained that to build a great crew, they select sailors who understand teamwork and know how to make a team work. They don't just look to recruit great sailors. They look for sailors that have experience of successful crews and how they operate. In doing so, they know that they are bringing knowledge and experience of teamworking into the crew, as well as sailing know-how. The crew then share this and draw on it as they begin to work together. This helps to accelerate the process of developing world-class teamwork within the crew.

What can we learn from rites of passage?

Many indigenous cultures have traditional rites of passage. These are often the dividing lines between childhood and adulthood: the point of transition at which a tribe accepts new members. In native tribes, the passage represents a change in social and cultural status for an individual. Samurai boys were presented with their adult clothes and haircut in their *Genpuku* ceremony. For young men particularly, the rite of passage often involved a test of skills, character and spiritual development. Lucullum Virgil McWhorter, a Native American Indian, describes his 'Vision Quest' – a tribal rite of passage.[6] Following a period of fasting, a young tribesman is required to journey alone into the wilderness for several days. This seclusion in nature provides him with a deep communication with the forces, spirits and energies of nature, and helps him to forge his self-identity. It is a journey that both develops and tests the youngster before they're enrolled within the tribe.

These rites of passage are common in indigenous cultures across the world. Many world-class teams also adopt this simple principle. They test potential recruits. To become a member of these teams, you must demonstrate your capability; you must qualify. The Red Arrows' recruitment process has several layers. As the Royal Air Force (RAF) aerobatic display team, recruits must first become RAF officers and then pilots. Only a select number of RAF pilots are invited to apply for the team each year. These hurdles need to be crossed before the potential recruit even makes it to Cyprus for the final selection.

The SAS employ an incredibly demanding set of physical and mental endurance tests, spanning a six-month period. These tests are designed to assess extreme abilities in a number of very functional skills, such as navigation, survival, combat skills and combat fitness. These are conducted in all weathers, night and day, in challenging terrains such as mountains and jungles, while carrying heavy loads. At the end of the process, those who successfully complete the tests are awarded the sand-coloured beret and stable belt of 'The Regiment'.

Brendan Hall describes how he was selected to skipper one of the Clipper Round the World Yacht Race crews. He said, 'The selection process to become a skipper involved an interview, plus a tough three-day skipper trial on the boat with simulated disasters. They wanted to know how we would respond and perform under pressure. We were tested relentlessly.'

Tough tests select those who *really* want to belong

Why, then, do these great teams test and qualify their recruits? Perhaps the most obvious reason is simply to ensure that they get the people who can do the job. Their tests are designed to allow potential recruits to demonstrate that they have the qualities necessary to be successful. However, there are other important reasons. By using tough tests, these organisations ensure that those who apply have a burning desire to become part of the team. Simply by enduring the tests, the applicants for the SAS are showing a strong desire to belong to the team. The candidates know that the success rate is extremely low: only a handful make it. In the summer of 2013, three soldiers died during the tests.[7]

Just filling in the application form requires a huge level of commitment. Despite all the hurdles they place in the way, the very best teams still have more applicants than places.

By qualifying new recruits, they also give current members the knowledge that everyone who joins their team has been thoroughly tested. SAS team members know just how tough the selection process is, having been through the experience themselves. Therefore, they have an inherent level of respect for anyone else who has made the grade. They know that they can depend on each other when it counts. If you were going into an operation behind enemy lines, I'm sure you'd want to go in knowing, not hoping, that your teammates were up to the task.

How can we test recruits?

Does this mean we should all send our potential recruits alone into the wilderness, or put them through combat tests in the jungles of Brunei? Perhaps not. I suspect that those particular tests will not tell you a great deal about whether a candidate is going to be right for your organisation. However, there are ways that we can all test potential recruits using the same basic formula that world-class teams use:

1 Create a situation that provides a tough challenge and which tests the attributes that you're looking for.

2 Observe the response.

The Mental Toughness Matrix

I was thrown a challenge recently by a world-leading sports team. The team wanted to identify whether potential signings were likely to be a good psychological fit for the team. The head of sport science asked me if I knew of an inventory or questionnaire that they could use to assess this. I told him that, to date, I hadn't found one. Instead, I tend to create specific challenges and a bespoke tool to record how players respond to the challenge. One such tool is known as The Mental Toughness

▶

Matrix and was originally designed for a US soccer organisation. The idea is very simple. We created a series of situations for the players, which tested their mental toughness. For example, we might give them a challenge that was right on the edge of their skills, increasing the likelihood that they would make mistakes, fail or lose. Asking people to perform when they are tired also increased the likelihood of errors, poor decision-making and emotional swings. Equally, we could expose them to hostile environments. We might put them in a situation where they received negative feedback or criticism. Occasionally we would disrupt their preparation, present them with unexpected changes or put them under time pressures. Could they adapt? To spice things up, we also gave them 'impossible' challenges. Then, we would note how the players responded.

The Mental Toughness Matrix simply allowed coaches, physiotherapists, trainers and support staff to record what they'd seen and heard. We identified six key elements of mental toughness and then described what responses we would see in players who were 'not so tough', 'slightly tough', 'getting tougher', 'pretty tough' and 'really tough'. The matrix helped us all to assess the six elements of toughness in the same way. After putting the players through various challenges, and recording our collective observations, we had a good idea about the level of mental toughness in these players.

Once you know what you are looking for, it becomes relatively easy to devise the tests and find ways to assess the response.

The best teams become a magnet for talent

Why do people go through these hugely demanding tests, knowing that only a small percentage will be successful? One very simple answer is because the organisation has become a magnet for talent. It's not surprising that people aspire to join the very best teams in the world. Many soldiers will dream about becoming a member of the SAS, just as pilots dream of flying in the fabled red flying suit of the Red Arrows. A New Zealander once told me that, 'Every Kiwi boy grows up wanting to play for the All Blacks.' These teams are recognised as 'the best'. By becoming a part of these teams, we identify ourselves as one of 'the best'. This very fundamental human desire helps to give great teams this magnetic quality.

Although that seems perfectly logical, it leaves us with some questions. How do I create an organisation that is a magnet for talent? Is this not a chicken-and-egg situation? Surely I need the talent in order to become the best.

If we dig a little deeper, it's possible to see more of the picture. The very best people often have other motives as well. They tend to look for audacious challenges and other people who share their ambitions. Those who want to be the very best that they can be, will seek out others who are on the same journey and who have the same mind-set. History shows us examples of teams that became the best by attracting great people. When those people joined the team, it was not yet 'the best'. Equally, the people may not have been 'the best' when they joined. However, what they did have was a genuine desire to make the journey together – an alignment in their vision. The team believed in the people and the people believed in the team.

As we look back on these teams we might be tempted to conclude that they had achieved because they were composed of world-class individuals. Rock bands such as U2 are good examples. When they formed, none of the members were world-class musicians. Their shared vision and ambitions allowed them to grow together as individuals and to become a world-class team.

World Cup-winning rugby coach Sir Clive Woodward describes how he optimised the performance of the players he had in order to drive the team's performance.[8] As the team began to perform, it became attractive to higher-quality players. In doing so, Clive took an ordinary team and created a magnet for talent.

Be prepared that you will sometimes recruit the wrong people

Do world-class organisations always recruit the perfect people, first time, every time? In my experience, the answer is no. In truth, they make mistakes too.

If you've ever watched children learning to walk, you'll notice that they fall over – a lot. Falling over is a very necessary part of the learning process. Mistakes are valuable. Even the very best teams on earth who apply the most demanding tests might not always recruit the perfect people first time. It's highly likely that you won't recruit the perfect person every time either. Knowing this, it seems wise to embrace the fact. What will you do when you realise the person you just recruited isn't a great fit? How will you know if the person you've recruited is right for you? What do you do if you suspect that they may not be a great fit? Do you hope they will change, or try to make the best of the situation? I have seen a lot of organisations that opt for one or both of those. It won't surprise you to know that world-class teams employ very different solutions.

We tend to learn far more about people once they are in the team than we do during the recruitment process. It's relatively easy for human beings to present a façade for short periods of time, but much more difficult to do it continuously. As a result, we all tend to revert to type after a while. Although you may get to see the real person in the first couple of weeks, it's more likely that their true nature will become apparent after the initial honeymoon period. This is the time when great leaders and teams become most aware. They'll cue into the subtle signs that tell them if their new recruit is likely to perform. Sometimes the evidence shows us that we have not found a good match. Rather than hoping that it will sort itself out, or trying to make the best of it, great teams and leaders act quickly. They may decide to bring the new recruit up to speed quickly. They'll set them some challenges and see whether they respond positively. Do they make progress? Are they willing to up their game and do what's necessary to be successful in the role? If not, maybe it's wise to admit that the relationship isn't going to work, and try again. Although this often means an uncomfortable conversation, it is also likely to be the fairest decision for both parties. Nobody likes to feel like they're struggling, or that they're letting the team down. Rather than persisting and creating misery, it's often best to agree that this probably isn't the best place for the recruit.

As teams review the performance of new recruits, they also sharpen their understanding of what 'the right people' look like. World-class teams are always learning. Rather than viewing it as a failure, they'll tend to learn the lessons and ensure that they refine their process next time.

The art of selection

'Selection wins or loses you more matches than anything else.'
Sir Clive Woodward[9]

Team selection is at the heart of an elite sport coach's role. The media, commentators and fans alike will often unpick and debate the coach's selection. Whichever team the coach selected, the fans could have done it better!

Of course, the challenges of team selection are not limited to sports. How do businesses select their executive leadership team? How are surgical teams selected? What about NASA shuttle crews or International Space Station (ISS) crews? How are project teams selected for specific tasks within organisations? Do we simply identify the roles and skills that are required and appoint individuals who can provide them? Will that give us a world-class team – or is there more to it than that? If we look in more detail at the way elite sports coaches and leaders select teams, we can see some of the principles that underpin their selection decisions and how we might be able to adopt them.

Chris Bartle is the head coach of the multiple-gold-medal-winning German Olympic Equestrian Team. He explained some of the considerations that underpin his selection decisions. Equestrian sports are built on partnerships, primarily those between horses and their riders. Chris is acutely aware that he needs to select partnerships rather than just riders.

Before the Beijing Olympics, he spent a great deal of time finding out which of the horses would be best suited to the environment. How would the animals respond to the humid climate, the demands of travelling, the terrain and the course? Chris knows that good decisions are often based on good information. To get the answers to these questions, the German squad sent a range of different horses to Hong Kong (the competition venue at the 2008 Olympics) to see how they responded. Each of the horses had different characteristics: different sizes, breeds, and so on. The results showed the team which types of horse were most likely to perform in those specific conditions.

Once they knew how the horses were likely to respond, Chris needed to consider the riders. He explained that he will not necessarily choose the five best riders, because they may not perform well as a team. Although each competitor rides alone, the interaction between them is critical. The order in which they ride is also important. For example, the first rider in the team is known as 'the pathfinder'. It is their job not only to ride well but also to gather information on the course, which helps the rest of the team to maximise their performance. In order to decide which five riders to select, and which roles to assign, Chris needs to know the athletes inside out. He spends a great deal of time learning about their characters and personalities, as well as their skills as athletes.[10]

Pinpoint the thought processes behind the best selection principles

On some occasions, it's possible to get an insight into the thought process behind selection decisions. Some sports, for example, have touring teams. Every four years, the British and Irish Lions rugby team tour for five to six weeks, playing 10–12 games in total. It is also traditional to have a three-game test series against the host nation at the culmination of the tour. As a result, the selection for these test matches becomes a significant focus for both the tour party and the watching public. Who will make the test team? Which players are on form? Which partnerships are working?

Is it simply a case of finding the best player for each position and throwing them onto the field together? Although that might be the case with some teams, the very best in the world use a more comprehensive process. In many cases, the coach looks to create a balanced team. Obviously, each team is made up of position specialists, but many coaches will also look to ensure that there is a balance between experienced operators and those who are new to the team. There is real value in having both those with experience and those who have the fresh perspective that comes with naivety. England's football team have seen the benefit that young, fearless faces bring. Some of the world's best coaches also take time to ensure that the blend of experience and new blood is interspersed throughout the team. This helps to avoid having pockets of inexperience. In rugby, this could mean that the coaching team will take time to assess the overall experience of the units within the team, such as the front row, back row, half-backs or back three.

Do we have combinations that work well together and

complement each other? Do we have personalities that can pull the various units together well and become the links between them? Do the team members make each other's lives easier or more difficult?

Aim for balance in the team

A team also needs to ensure it is balanced in other ways. Leadership is a prime example. Experience and leadership don't always go hand in hand. The experienced members are not always the best leaders, and vice versa. The coach needs to know how the players are likely to respond in various situations. Who is likely to step up and lead in adversity and how will they lead? Who will provide the direction? Who can change the strategy on the field, when necessary? Is the person who detects the need for a change also the person who can best adapt the plan and communicate it? The coach may also need to consider the likely scenarios that will occur within a game and select players who will tend to cope better.

Creating a balanced team also means identifying possible imbalances. Do we have a balance between the dependable players and the risk takers? Do we have both those with calm heads and those mavericks with the 'fire'? Is there a balance between the intuitive, instinctive players and the calculating, analytical players? Do we have a balance between the predictable and the unpredictable, the creative and the steady? What is the mix of personalities in the team? Do we have the balance that we need?

Choose a team that can rise to the particular challenge

In addition to all these considerations, a coach will also need to ensure that they select a team that can best meet the demands of the immediate challenge. In sport, there are always contextual factors. One of the most obvious is the opposition. What game plan do we need to give ourselves the best chance of success?

There are also environmental factors such as the climate and conditions. In 2013, the British and Irish Lions kicked off their tour in the heat and humidity of Hong Kong. They faced a Barbarians team that contained a host of world superstars that had only been together for a week or two. Therefore, the game plan to face the Barbarians was very different from the one employed against Australia in the first test.

Which team is best equipped to execute the game plan and therefore give us the best chance of success?

The consequences of unbalanced teams

What happens if we don't have balance within the team? In many cases the answers might be relatively obvious. If we have an inexperienced team, we are likely to see some unusual decision-making. Inexperienced teams tend to experiment during critical moments rather than sticking to a tried-and-tested game plan. An inexperienced team is also likely to be on a steep learning curve. Although they may be brilliant on some occasions, they also have the potential to be quite erratic. If we haven't got the right balance of skills, we might be great in some areas of our performance but struggle in others. This, in turn, could limit the game plan that we're able to execute. Sometimes we may need to adapt our game plan so that we maximise our strengths and try to reduce the exposure of our weaker areas.

However, there are imbalances that might not be as immediately obvious. What if we have both the skills and experience but we have an imbalance in the personality profiles of our team? In Chapter 1, I briefly discussed the different personality types and their tendencies. Here's a very basic view of the four dominant personality types loosely based on the ones that Carl Jung identified,[11] and presented in my own way for ease of understanding. The descriptions show the extremes of these personalities, so as to illustrate the differences. We are not exclusively one of these types. Everyone is a blend, and therefore has all these different tendencies to varying degrees. You'll probably look at this list and see something of yourself in each category. In reality, we are a concoction of these personality types, with a dominant type, secondary, tertiary and least dominant type.

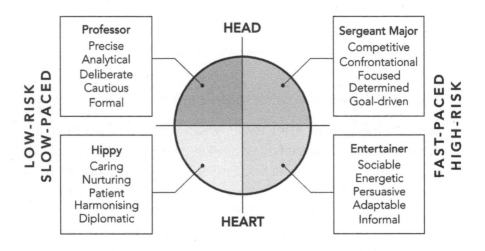

The personality types

Just for interest, what do you think your dominant personality type is? Are you primarily a 'sergeant major', an 'entertainer', a 'hippy' or a 'professor'? What would you say your secondary, tertiary and least dominant type is?

Now, let's think of how all this affects the make-up of a team. What happens if our team is made up primarily of professors and hippies? If the team is imbalanced towards the left half of this table, your team will probably be slow to respond and make decisions. It is also less likely to take risks and therefore may miss opportunities. On the other hand, if your team is over-balanced to the right half of the table, you are likely to be impulsive and hasty, rather than measured and strategic. Alternatively, if a team has more 'head' than 'heart' it might not respond intuitively or may even distance itself because it appears not to take regard of people's feelings. A team that is 'head' strong might not fully understand the emotional impact of a decision. Conversely, a team with more 'heart' than 'head' tends not to make calculated decisions and is inclined to go with its gut-feeling.

The professors and hippies in the team often provide the hand brake and will slow down a decision. They like to make sure that we have all the information and think things through thoroughly. These are tremendously valuable qualities. The sergeant majors provide much-needed direction and urgency, while the hippies give us harmony and diplomacy, diffusing conflict and keeping a team together. The entertainers will get things moving and be happy working with vague concepts, chaos and uncertainty. They are also likely to provide the out-of-the-box thinking. Often I find that the entertainers are great at getting things started but not so great at completing and finishing. The professors, on the other hand, struggle with vague ideas and concepts. Once an idea has some form and structure, they can refine it, complete it and finish it. In balanced teams, these different attributes work together really well. If there is an imbalance and one of these elements is missing, the team tends to struggle.

Getting things done well

While working with a research and development team, I began to appreciate the importance of having the right personality blend within the team. This particular team of engineers was primarily composed of 'sergeant majors' and 'professors'. Their task was to produce a prototype that best met the design brief that they had been given. Of course, they had

▶

a deadline to hit as well. Left to their own devices, the sergeant majors would hit the deadline, although the quality of the prototype was not always wonderful. The professors, on the other hand, would tend to produce a fantastic prototype but often missed the deadlines. The most successful team contained both personality types and it drew on the strengths of each type. As a result it consistently produced the best possible prototype by the deadline.

FIFA World Cup referee Howard Webb described how his team of three contained a balanced approach. In the trio, Howard provided energy and direction while his two assistant referees provided the analytical skills and the diligence to follow things through.

Select for continuity

Did you know that the Manchester United treble-winning football team of 1998/9 played 63 competitive games in various competitions during that season? Their squad comprised of 38 players, 29 of whom started games for the first team. Of these 29, 8 of the squad started 40 or more games together and another 4 players made more than 30 appearances. These eight core players included the goalkeeper (Peter Schmeichel), three defenders (Denis Irwin, Gary Neville and Jaap Stam), two midfielders (David Beckham and Roy Keane) and two forwards (Dwight Yorke and Andy Cole). This small group of players were the nucleus of the team and provided the continuity on which the performance was built. Of course, this didn't happen by chance. It was a result of the manager's selection decisions.

Was Manchester United's success during the 1998/9 season a

fluke, or was it perhaps influenced by the level of continuity that existed within the playing squad? This pattern extended beyond the 1998/9 season. For several years they had a stable core group of playing staff and support staff. The manager, coaching staff, medical staff and the leaders on the field had all been working together for several seasons. Many of the fringe players had been developed through the Academy system, so they had become accustomed to the culture, the style of play, the coaching and the management. If we look at teams across a variety of disciplines, it is common to see that success and continuity often go hand in hand. It's reasonable to expect that, in order to perform well together, the team need time together. Team members need time to become familiar with each other, to understand how each other makes decisions and the way they respond. Often teams that perform together for many years will also evolve together and learn how to adapt to the changes around them.

'Successful crews are built through time on the water together.'
Andy Beadsworth, America's Cup Helmsman

Naturally, this principle extends beyond football and sport. It's unlikely that organisations that have a revolving door will deliver consistently high-quality performances.

Summary

Getting the right people in the right place at the right time is central to the performance of most teams. Recruiting those who are a good fit for both the organisation and the role is a fundamental starting point. These might not be the most talented people, but they will be the ones who will have the greatest positive impact on the performance of the team. Once we have the right people in the organisation, we need to construct teams that are balanced and designed for the task. Giving these teams time to become familiar and learn about each other, gives them every chance of developing the dynamics that allow them to perform.

- Do some background research on your prospective candidate. Ask some pointed questions to discover how the person responded during a tough season or a difficult work situation.

- Identify exactly what characteristics are required to be successful in the specific roles you're hiring for. Going with your gut-feeling might not cover all the necessary aspects, so compiling a set of criteria appropriate to your organisation could be more useful.

- In order to recruit 'a great team player' you need to know exactly what one looks like, sounds like and behaves like. Look for those who have experience of successful teamwork and how they operate, rather than just being great at their job.

- Think about using tests where potential recruits can demonstrate that they possess the necessary qualities you are seeking.

- If your decision turns out to be less successful than expected, set some challenges to see whether the new recruit responds positively. If he or she does not, be honest and be prepared to part.

- Become a magnet for talent. Remember, talented people are often looking for those who share their vision, ambition and values.

- Look for balance and understand the types of personalities and how they can affect the operations of your team: do the team members have personalities that can pull together well and make each other's lives easier – or more difficult? Good decisions are often based on good information.

WORKSHOP: Recruitment and selection

How would you rate your recruitment and selection? Take a moment to look at the following elements and score how well you apply them using the simple 0–10 scale. As before, a score of 10 means 'perfect, flawless, cannot be improved'. A score of zero means that there is nothing good about it.

1 Do you know what the 'perfect person' looks like?
2 Do you test potential recruits?
3 How well do you deal with the situation if you recruited the wrong person?
4 Are you becoming a magnet for talent?
5 Do you select balanced teams?
6 Are the teams you select well matched to the challenge?
7 Do you create continuity through selection?

What can you do to improve your score by just one? See 'What Can You Learn?' on page 12 and use the summary above to guide you through the basic elements that can help you improve your recruitment and selection techniques.

CHAPTER 3

Great Team Players

In Chapter 2, we discovered that the Red Arrows don't recruit the *best three pilots* each year to join the team. Instead, they recruit the *best team players*. As we learned, the Red Arrows understand that we can often identify team players by the choices they make. A great team player chooses to take responsibility and chooses to commit to the team and align to team goals. Of course, these are not the only characteristics of a great team player.

During the last five years, I have worked with a number of the world's best adventure racers. Adventure racing, if you haven't come across it before, is an extreme team sport. The teams of four must contain at least one male and one female. These teams race each other for several days in the wilderness. Bruce Duncan captained the British team to three consecutive victories in the Wenger Patagonian Expedition race: a mammoth 600km race through the Chilean Andes. The event is a type of triathlon, comprising trekking, mountain biking and kayaking. Each team is required to carry their kit with them. The winning British team typically take around six days to complete the race, sometimes sleeping for as little as 15 hours. It's no surprise that it is known as the toughest team race on the planet.

Robyn Benincasa has also completed over 40 multi-day adventure races. Like Bruce, she is acutely aware that adventure racing is a team challenge. 'Some people would say that if they get to the finish line, as an individual, they're successful. I don't subscribe to that. If we get to the finish line, we're successful.'

Team players are willing to help each other – and be helped

Robyn and Bruce know that there are always times when somebody in the team will reach a low point. In fact, during the race, everyone will hit the bottom at some point. When it happens, the team need to pick that person up and take some of their load. Great team players are always willing to help carry someone else's bag. Now, that's not a particularly earthshattering revelation. Crucially, Robyn and Bruce know that the flip side is also true: great team players are also willing to let other people carry their bags.

Although many athletes are willing to help others, they can be too proud to let somebody else help them. In adventure racing, this can have a very detrimental effect on the team. When people get tired, they slow down. The team's aim is to complete the course as quickly as possible, so slowing down doesn't help. Those who are too proud to let others carry their bag inevitably slow the team down. As we get tired, our decision-making also tends to become compromised. Many people's mood becomes negative, which can also have a negative impact on the team. Obviously, this is not just true in adventure racing. I'm sure you'll have seen examples of people who were unwilling to accept help and, as a consequence, slowed their team down.

Robyn Benincasa's formula for great team players is pretty simple: 'No ego. No blame.'

No ego

Before exploring how great team players operate with no ego, it's probably wise to understand what we mean by the term 'ego'.

One dictionary defines ego as, 'the "I" or self of any person; a person as thinking, feeling, and willing, and distinguishing itself from the selves of others and from objects of its thought'.[1]

In this context, I am not suggesting that great team players have no sense of themselves, and that they cease to be thinking, feeling and willing individuals capable of distinguishing themselves from others. Interestingly, further definitions of the term 'ego' also reveal that it is, 'one's image of oneself'. It is this understanding of ego that leads us to talk of 'boosting our ego'. I tend to think of the ego as the part of our psyche concerned with how we present ourselves, how we'd like others to see us, and what we'd like them to think of us.

Have you ever noticed yourself thinking, *I need to look good here*, or *I really don't want to look bad*? When our ego dominates, we might become concerned about how other people perceive us. This state of thinking can impact on our decision-making. For many years, I have worked in elite professional sports clubs. It's not uncommon to see players making decisions to protect the way they look, or more specifically how they perceive others will view them, at the expense of the team. There are a variety of reasons for this. It might be that they are aware of how they will be portrayed in the media. Equally, they might have ambitions to represent their country. In these situations, players may not opt to push the limits and risk making a mistake, even though the team might need them to.

Cricket is a game that is dominated by statistics. Batsmen are often judged on their *average*. This is the total number of runs that they have scored, divided by the number of times they have been dismissed. A batsman could easily choose to play it safe and protect their average, rather than take riskier shots that might help their team score as many runs as possible.

In an interview with BBC Sport, winning British and Irish Lions coach Sir Ian McGeechan described the importance of having players who are prepared to invest in the team.

> What you don't want is egos. You need someone who is prepared to put everything they have into the jersey and, as support staff, we have to make it as easy as possible for every player to feel that way. If the players all feel that way, then you have an environment to have success in the Test matches.
>
> In 1997, we won the first Test in Cape Town and we were heading out for dinner. Jonno [captain Martin Johnson] got up on the bus on the way to the restaurant – everyone was excited after the win – and he just said: 'We are a team and we have to prepare for a game on Tuesday night. The Test team will be there at 9 o'clock in the morning to hold the tackle bags.'
>
> Not one player was late to get on the bus. You know then that you have the right environment, and the players understand what it is to be a Lion.[2]

It is a very similar philosophy to that adopted by the All Blacks. They use a technical term: no dickheads. As their mental skills coach, Gilbert Enoka, explains,

> Ego has to be left at the door; there is a rigidly enforced 'no dickhead policy' in the squad and every player takes turns in sweeping the changing room clean after each game.
>
> The jersey can hunt out flaws as quickly as you can look at it. The dickheads and the posers who are not genuine about adding to this wonderful legacy just don't survive ... They become one-Test ponies and get chewed up and spat out relatively quickly.[3]

How does this apply to you?

Of course, this phenomenon is not just seen in sport. I have witnessed many discussions in boardroom environments where company directors seem more intent on winning the argument than finding the best solution. Daft as it sounds, I have also seen sales executives stealing business from their colleagues in an attempt to hit their own targets and top the leader board. Although this mentality might seem different from an adventure racer's reluctance to let someone else carry their bag, it emanates from the same thought process. The adventure racer who refuses help is making a statement in an attempt to hide a weakness from others, or to appear strong. The director who seeks to win the argument wants to appear smart, or avoid looking dumb. The sales executive wants to finish top of the leader board to look successful and avoid looking like a failure.

Of course, all these decisions are driven by our insecurities.

No blame

The second element of Robyn Benincasa's formula is 'no blame'. Our tendency to blame circumstances and other people also stems from our ego and our insecurities. In his book, *Managing Yourself and Others*, Australian sport psychologist Phil Jauncey argues that many people suffer from a modern-day cultural disease; they believe that it's OK to fail as long as they feel good about it.[4] Rather than looking for ways to address the issues that are causing them to fail, they look instead for excuses. In blaming something external, we attempt to deceive ourselves. We try to hide behind the notion that our situation is the result of something outside our control. I suspect that we do this to protect our ego. Our ego doesn't like to think we are at fault.

Through our ego, we are likely to judge our self. Negative self-judgement usually stings. To avoid the discomfort, therefore, we often choose to find an excuse. We choose to ease the immediate sensation of pain, rather than take responsibility.

This challenge is exacerbated if we're feeling low on confidence. If we perceive that we're failing, and we feel the sting of self-judgement, our natural tendency might be to make an excuse or to blame. If we feel that we're in a vulnerable position, the easiest and most comfortable option is to look to external reasons. Ironically, these are the times when it is most important to take responsibility.

Blame and excuses can often be accompanied by defensiveness, anger and guilt. Therefore, those who also become angry and defensive may also become a real negative influence on their team.

Talented but struggling

I have recently been working with a professional sports team that is widely regarded as one of the best teams in the world in its sport. It is normal for our team to contain numerous international players. On occasions, our players will take time away from the club to play for their country. It is, of course, a great honour for them and for the club. However, it is not uncommon for these players to struggle when they return from international duty.

Historically, while they are away with the international team, these players have encountered a great deal of scrutiny and judgement. This has come both from the international coaching team and from the media. As you can imagine, the media spotlight is intensified on the international stage. Players can end up

▶

feeling as if their every move is being monitored, critiqued and judged. The result is that they can begin to become defensive.

We tend to notice that this defensiveness accompanies the players as they come back into the club. Initially they react adversely to critical feedback and sometimes get angry. I suspect that their ego combines their status as 'international players' with their exposure to the hypercritical environment. This can become compounded if they struggled to perform in the international team. They begin to use blame to protect their own view of themselves. Ironically, their attempts to look good by deflecting the blame end up having the opposite effect. Their club-mates see their negativity, hear them blaming, making excuses and moaning. Of course, these behaviours are not what their fellow players associate with great teammates.

Surrender 'I' for 'we'

Focus follows interest. If we are overly focused on ourselves, we're not likely to be focused on our team.

In his book, *Sacred Hoops*, Chicago Bulls basketball coach Phil Jackson emphasises the importance of inspiring his players to become acutely aware of what is happening, even when the spotlight is on somebody else.[5] In his words, 'Selflessness is the soul of teamwork.' To create a great basketball team, Phil Jackson knew that his players needed to be utterly aware of, and in tune with, the other players. He would ask his players, 'If you are on the bench, are you awake and in tune?' To do this, they must be focused on each other, not purely on themselves.

In order to immerse into a team, we must allow ourselves to become absorbed by it. Rather than holding on to our identity as an individual, we must be happy to lose ourselves into our collective identity as a team. We must place more importance on our contribution and belonging to 'we' than to 'me'. It requires us to focus on 'me as a part of us', not just as 'me'.

Of course, this can be difficult for some. If we build our self-worth on our successes as an individual, we might be reluctant to fuse our individual identity into the collective identity of the team. Therefore, an athlete who defines him or herself by their personal performance might well be less willing to immerse themselves in the team. Naturally, this phenomenon isn't limited to athletes. I have observed the same in executives, surgeons, lawyers, politicians and academics, to name but a few.

The wisdom of Socrates

Socrates implored us to 'know thyself'. It is a simple message. However, I would argue that very few people today have a deep knowledge of themselves. It may also seem contradictory to suggest that great team players are selfless while also emphasising the importance of self-knowledge. Our ability to know ourselves is crucial if we are to become self-comfortable and therefore less invested in our ego. Those who are comfortable in their own skin feel less need to prove anything or to create an image of themselves for others. They don't need to define themselves by their individual performance or successes. Therefore the combination of self-knowledge and authenticity is incredibly powerful. When we know ourselves, and feel comfortable being ourselves, we are able to operate in an ego-less way and therefore to invest ourselves in the team.

Those who are self-comfortable are also less likely to blame situations and other people when they make mistakes. They'll feel happy to take responsibility, be self-critical and seek critical input from others. If we think back to the Red Arrows, and what they look for in team players, we see that they select those who are comfortable choosing to take responsibility, and who will accept criticism and align with team goals. Although it might seem contrary, our ability to be self-comfortable and secure allows us to become a better team player.

Why invest in the team?

Phil Jackson explains that there needs to be a reason why National Basketball Association (NBA) players would want to invest in the team performance. Traditionally, NBA players have made their names as individuals. He describes the challenge of getting players to play for the team rather than showcasing their individual skills. He recognised that many NBA players saw fame and fortune following those superstars that displayed the greatest individual flair on court. Phil Jackson's challenge at the Bulls was to help Michael Jordan, who was arguably the greatest individual player in history, to understand the benefits of playing *for* the team rather than just *in* the team. When Michael Jordan focused on helping the team perform at its best, their collective success was unprecedented. Interestingly, the success that the Bulls subsequently enjoyed as an organisation may also have helped Jordan himself to attain his legendary status as a player.

Phil Jackson also focused the team on appreciating that being part of 'the dance' is more fulfilling. In his experience, and that of many other players, a personal victory can be empty compared to winning as a team.

Ask yourself:

- Why should team members invest in the team?

- What's the compelling reason – the strong, clear, shared purpose?

- Why does it matter?

- Why will you be stronger together?

- How will team members benefit from investing themselves in this team?

Summary

In order to recruit and develop great team players, we need to know what they look like, sound like and behave like. How do you spot a great team player? World-class organisations understand that we identify team players through their behaviours and their choices. We can see and hear the difference between those who choose to take responsibility and those who moan or apportion blame. Equally, we can spot those who ask for help when they need it and those who are too proud to seek support. In fact, when you look for them, the signs become more obvious. Once we know what kind of people make great team players, encouraging our team-members to adopt those characteristics also becomes much easier.

- Great team players are always willing to help 'carry someone else's bag', either literally or figuratively, and will also allow other members to do the same for them when needed. Those who are too proud to let others help them inevitably slow the team down.

- Where there is no ego, there is no blame. Our decision-making can be affected if we are too involved in ourselves and how others perceive us. In the work situation it might be someone attempting to hide a weakness by trying to win an argument or appearing smart.

- When they fail, rather than looking for excuses, effective team players will look at their own actions. Excuses and blame tend to go with defensiveness, anger and guilt, which are negative influences on the team.

- Team members need to be able to lose their personal identity and put more emphasis on the contribution they are making to the team. They need to be completely aware of, and in tune with, the other players.

- Remember that those who are self-comfortable are also less likely to blame situations and other people when they make mistakes.

WORKSHOP: Great team players

Reflect on what you see in your team at the moment. Take a moment and score your team using the simple 0–10 scale. As before, a score of 10 means 'perfect, flawless, cannot be improved'. A score of zero means that there is nothing good about it.

How willing are your people to:

1 Take responsibility?
2 Align to team goals?
3 Ask for help when they need it and allow others to 'carry their bag'?
4 Put the team before the needs of their own ego?
5 Play *for* the team, rather than just *in* the team?

What can you do to improve your score for each by just one? See 'What Can You Learn?' on page 12 and use the summary above to suggest ways to improve the way your team players work together. Now answer the following question: why should your people invest in the team?

CHAPTER 4

World-class Teamwork

Why is it that some teams seem to have a telepathic understanding of each other? Their actions appear to be seamlessly blended; like a flock of starlings or a shoal of herring moving together as one. How are teams able to do this? What can leaders do to develop teams that are capable of this mesmerising synchronicity? How is it that they are able to communicate with a fleeting glance, a wink or a nod of the head? What's the secret to their incredible level of understanding? Equally, some teams appear to have super-strong bonds. In some cases, their members are literally willing to put their lives on the line for each other. How do leaders develop this intense loyalty within their teams?

When we see these teams in action, it's possible to think that these characteristics are somehow inherent. Is it possible to develop teams like this, or do they form almost by chance? Are they shaped by the situations and circumstances that surround them? It seems reasonable that a team of soldiers are willing to die for each other, because their circumstance dictates that they face life-threatening situations. Is it possible, then, to develop super-strong bonds without throwing the team into a war-zone?

While working with, and studying, world-class teams and leaders at work, I have discovered some of the mechanisms that enable world-class teamwork. Experience has shown me that great teamwork is not inherent, accidental or purely the result of circumstance. There are some fundamental elements that allow teams to deliver world-class performances, which we can all apply to our own teams.

Why have a team?

An investment banker asked me, during a recent event, how he could get his traders to work as a team. He described the environment as a 'dog-eat-dog world', where the traders were entirely focused on themselves and their own performance, with no regard for the team. My response was to ask him, 'Why do they need to be a team?' He was a little taken aback initially, and probably wondered why I'd asked such a strange question. Surely all groups of individuals should work as a team, right? As we got chatting, I asked him why these traders should work collaboratively. What was the benefit in working together? Would it help them to achieve their targets? Would it make their lives easier? Was there a reason why they would benefit from working as a team, rather than as a collection of individuals under the same brand and with some shared resources? These were questions that the investment banker struggled to answer. Interestingly, as the conversation progressed, it became obvious that he wanted them to be a team because he carried the title of 'team leader'. Therefore, there was a default expectation that they should operate as a collective. In reality though, the rationale for the team was not as obvious.

It stands to reason that there has to be a compelling reason for the team to exist. Creating a high-performing team can be hard work, which requires time, effort and focus from its members. In order for people to immerse themselves in the team and invest in it, there needs to be a strong and clear rationale. We often think of individuals serving the team, but how does the team serve the individuals? Many great teams actually help the members to realise their ambitions. One of the sports teams that I work with places considerable importance on helping the players to become the best that they can be individually and collectively. The club knows that it can make a significant contribution to this. They know that the players want to achieve their potential and play at the highest possible level. They understand that players want to win championships and represent their country. Therefore, the club has become acutely aware of the value that the team has for the players, as well as the value that the players bring to the team.

Why would team members 'put their lives on the line' for each other?

Why is it that some team members are willing to put their lives on the line for their team? It appears that there are two fundamental factors. The first is that the team has an incredibly strong and compelling purpose – one that is worth dying for. Members of the Special Forces are often acutely aware that their mission is critically important. If they fail, the consequences could be catastrophic. On one level, they know that failure could mean that their teammates don't survive. However, they also know that there are many others whose fate rests with them. The success of a Special Forces mission could also affect hundreds or thousands of military personnel. If an SAS unit is unable to destroy enemy missile positions, many other lives will be put at risk. Beyond the military personnel, there are potentially millions of innocent civilians who also depend on the success of the mission. It is not hard to see that having a strong and compelling reason is fundamentally important.

The second factor is the level of loyalty that team members have for each other. Crucially, the team members have to care about each other in order to put their lives on the line for their comrades. Although you might be thinking that teams like this are rare, I suspect you see them every day. Family units are (sometimes) shining examples of teams in which people would willingly put their life on the line for each other. They do so because they care deeply about their teammates. In fact, I've often heard the members of great teams referring to their teammates as brothers and sisters.

What lies behind a team that cares for each other?

How do we develop this intense loyalty and care for each other? Do we simply arrange more team nights out? Do we all need to be friends? Personally, I'm not sure that team nights out will do the job entirely. I would also suggest that even the closest of family units might not like each other sometimes. However, they do care deeply! A British Army corporal described the way that his company would 'eat together, drink together and sleep together'. They were immersed in each other's company. Although they didn't always get on, or agree, they developed a deep understanding of each other. They began to know each other. They became aware of how each other would respond in different situations, and how they were likely to feel.

As well as this knowledge, they also began to build a 'bank of gratitude' with each other. You may have said the words, 'Thanks, I owe you one', as you're building relationships with those around you. We invest into our relationships by helping each other out and returning the favours. Each time we do so, we begin to appreciate each other and strengthen the bonds between us. If one of your teammates saved your life, you might pledge to help them, whatever it took and whenever they needed it. But, it's not only those momentous, life-and-death incidents that develop this intense loyalty. Even small acts enable us to invest into our relationships with others. Therefore, by understanding these simple principles, we can begin to see how we create a team of people who are willing to put themselves on the line for each other.

What happens when our teammates mean everything to us?

US Navy SEAL Team Leader, Gary Rossi, told me how his friend and colleague Michael E. Thornton risked his life to save his lieutenant, Tommy Norris:

'Mike was an engineman second class in the Navy during Vietnam. Mike and Tommy were working with the South Vietnamese (SV) SEALs, who had a reputation for not being the best in land navigation. The truth is, they got lost in there. Like typical blokes who don't ask for directions, they knew they were lost but kept on driving. They weren't supposed to come under any enemy fire whatsoever, and there were five of them.

'Anyway, because they were in the wrong place at the wrong time, they ran smack dab into a battalion of North Vietnamese Regulars. Of course a fire fight ensued. The way Mike says it, when they realised they were getting over-run, they withdrew. He was running with two of the SV SEALs and looked round and said, "Where's the lieutenant?" One of the SV SEALs said "Lieutenant dead, lieutenant dead."

'Now, our teammates are the most important thing in our lives. Since we operate in small units, we have to rely on each other. We have specific duties and responsibilities, and if one of us goes down, that's a big hit for the rest of us. Since the SEAL teams were first formed, we never leave our comrades behind – we have never left a teammate and not got him back, so Mike went back.

▶

'If I remember correctly, Mike got shot twice – in the shoulder and in the quadriceps. But he picked up Tom Norris. Tom got hit by a round in the back of his head, in the left-hand side. It's remarkable, but the round did not penetrate the skull and was deflected by the bone mass, around the top of the skull and came out just above his left eye. It basically blew his eye out. When Mike saw the injury, he was pretty convinced that Tommy was dead. However, he picked him up and carried him back to the beach.

'So, Mike had been wounded twice and was carrying Tom, running to the beach, before swimming – while towing his unconscious comrade – for two hours to the rendezvous.

'Mike knows that when you go into battle, you may not get out alive. Mike was thinking, *I'm not going to leave a teammate of mine. And when I get him out, I am going to do everything I can to save myself and save him.*'

It takes time to develop strong relationships

Interestingly, in the account above, Gary Rossi says, 'Our teammates are the most important thing in our lives.' It is possible that we forget the basic rules of human interaction when working in a team. I suspect that some people assume their team members should cooperate, should collaborate and should be loyal to each other simply because they are part of the same unit. In reality though, teams are built upon human relationships. I've witnessed many team-building sessions in which people recognise the need for trust, respect and sacrifice. These important words get scribbled on the flipchart sheets at the front of the room in colourful ink. However, it's rare that they are actually realised. Why should people trust each other and respect each other? Trust and respect don't just happen. Our relationships inside the team are fundamentally the same as those we have in the rest of our lives. In order to develop strong bonds, we have to want to put ourselves out for other people. We have to want to invest in our relationships. When we invest time and energy in someone else, we show them that they are important to us, and vice versa. Equally, when someone disregards something that we value, we question their ethics and question our trust in them. These human interactions are the building blocks of our relationships and therefore the foundations of teamwork.

Creating synchronicity

Have you ever watched a shoal of sardines moving almost as one to avoid a predator? They display an astonishing level of synchronicity. As the marlin dives towards the shoal, the mass of fish seems to create a void around their enemy and then seamlessly reform. It continually breaks and reforms, eluding the marlin. Looking at the shoal, it is tempting to view them as an amazing team. They seem to be governed by one mind. To the onlooker, it appears that they collectively decide how and where they move. However, the truth is that they don't think as a team at all. The sardines don't collectively decide to move in any given direction. Instead, they independently decide to do the same thing. Like flocks of starlings, the sardines actually function according to a few simple principles. One is to stay as close to the middle of the shoal as possible. Another is to get out the way of the predator. If the predatory marlin approached from the right, it's likely that the sardines would all individually opt to move to the left in order to escape. They also seek to be in the centre, which results in the shoal continually reforming. The reality is that each sardine makes an independent decision that is based on its own self-interest.

Incredibly, this gives the impression that they're making a collective decision.

How does this understanding help us to create a similar synchronicity in our teams?

The key point here is that the fish all respond to the same cues in the same way. Very simply, when X happens, I do Y. If we all adopt this principle, when X happens, we all do Y. This elementary mechanism also allows colonies of ants to coordinate the way they respond to changes in their environment. Ants are capable of an astonishing level of coordination, to the point where a colony is considered not to be a collection of individual ants but a super-organism. Much of the ant's sensory system is governed by aromas and pheromones. When they detect the changes in their environment, each ant has a predetermined response; when X happens, they do Y. Because all the ants operate in the same way, they present a collective response.

How a sailing crew synchronises

The same base principle used by ants and shoals of fish also allows elite yacht racing crews, including Americas Cup and Extreme 40s crews, to respond to changes in the wind, currents and race conditions, as helmsman Andy Beadsworth explained:

> Yacht racing is all about what you give away. The tiny little margins all add up. We might be able to gain 0.2 knots for 10 seconds because 10 people move 50cm together. Of course we're either in the process of losing or gaining momentum, so every little gain is important. Each decision gains or loses momentum. The ability to move everyone to the right that 50cm happens because the guy on 'the trim' [the crew member who 'trims' the sail to ensure that it is

the optimal size and shape to catch the wind] shouts '2–1–press!' Everyone knows that the call could come. It's not a surprise, so they listen out to 'the trim'.

The ability to respond quickly makes a huge difference on the water. A sail change, for example, might take 10 seconds. If we need to start the process from scratch it might not be worth doing before we hit the next mark, because it will happen too late, so we might decide to muddle through. A great team will know that a sail change is a possibility so will have prepared for it in advance. They'll have all the ropes ready, etc. They're looking for the signal to make the switch so that when I give it, the change happens quickly and we get the extra speed. Their awareness of the situation allows them to see the possibilities together and know what options they need to have available.

Rules ensure that each team member thinks as one

Each sailor on the crew understands that when there is a change in X, they need to do Y. However, it is not only yacht crews that adopt this principle. Red Arrows' team leader Jas Hawker explained that they follow a defined set of standard operating procedures (SOPs). These SOPs ensure that everyone works to the same base processes and that each team member understands how the team does things. In the Red Arrows it starts with flight planning, meteorological reports, briefings, preparing the aeroplanes, switching engines on and taxiing to the runway. Therefore, the SOPs lay the foundation for the way in which teammates operate and provide the basis for this common response.

Interestingly, this also happens on a more strategic and cultural level. Sir Clive Woodward explained that the England Rugby Team had a 'black book' that contained their teamship rules.[1] It was an incredibly valuable tool to help successfully induct new members to the squad. It explicitly laid down their expectations and codes of conduct. It was a written representation of their culture and their processes, and it explained 'how we do things around here'. Skipper Brendan Hall adopted a very similar approach with his Clipper Round the World Yacht Race crew.[2] One of their challenges was to integrate the core crew members (who sailed the entire global race) with leggers (new crew members who would sail specific legs). His crew created a very detailed guide for new members and ensured that when leggers joined the crew they spent time with core members to learn the ropes as quickly as possible.

Simply having a set of SOPs or a shared understanding isn't enough to create synchronicity, however. America's Cup helmsman Andy Beadsworth said that the ability to collectively respond to changes during the race is developed by spending time on the water together. Time on the water helps them to turn theory into practice. Crucially, it allows them to encounter challenges together and to find solutions. This process of planning, preparing and practising together allows them to become better at collectively finding solutions to challenges as they arise. By doing this, they begin to know how each member of the crew responds to changes in their environment.

Rethinking as situations arise – sailing in squalls

Skipper Brendan Hall describes how his crew learned to sail in dangerous conditions.

'Squalls are very powerful and dangerous localised winds. They hit very quickly, bringing wind up from almost nothing to 45 knots and can last from seconds to half an hour. They usually bring lashing rain, meaning that visibility drops to zero.

▶

Our challenge would be dropping our large, light wind sails before the squall hit and tore them to pieces. Once the squall had passed, we'd be left with no wind and would need to re-hoist our lightweight sails again.

'When we were first hit by a squall, we responded too late. The crew struggled to get the large sail down and it was flog-ging uncontrollably. The mast was shaking violently and I thought we were going to break something. It was dangerous. After that first incident I called a debrief. Squalls tend to be gen-erated by a single cloud or bank of clouds. We learned how to spot a potential squall and get into position early, so that we could wait there and drop the sail at the right moment. It greatly reduced the time it took to execute the manoeuvre, meaning that we could handle the squalls more safely and quickly.'

How does this apply to you?

Businesses have the opportunity to create synchronicity in their teams too. Business teams can develop the equivalent to 'time on the water' by continually taking on challenges as a team. In order to understand how they would respond to changes in their envi-ronment, an executive leadership team spent time collectively assessing how the world around them changed. The team iden-tified cues that they could all focus on and discussed their possible responses. Once they knew what to look for and listen to, and the options available to them, the team was able to coor-dinate a response much more quickly and effectively.

'In preparing for battle I have always found that plans
are useless, but planning is indispensable'
Dwight D. Eisenhower

How can you develop telepathic understanding?

Knowing how we need to respond to changes in our environment goes a long way to helping us create a more telepathic understanding. Of course, great teamwork is underpinned by great communication. World-class teams tend to communicate very differently from most. Contrary to popular opinion, I have noticed that, when it comes to communication, less is more!

America's Cup helmsman Andy Beadsworth explains: 'In a strong team there is little communication. Champion boats are often silent boats. The team is aware of the environment and we all know how we're likely to respond. We look to each other for certain cues. Sometimes all we need is eye contact to exchange a look. It might be to say that I'm under pressure here and I need you to help. As the skipper or helmsman, I may be able to slow the boat slightly and buy you some time. If I know when the pressure is likely to build, I know when to look at you to see how you're doing. I also know what I can do if I see you struggling. This is all developed through time on the water.'

Know each other's roles and share signals

FIFA World Cup referee Howard Webb described how his team work together. It starts by understanding each other's roles intimately. They are focused on each other and they deliberately look for times when a colleague might struggle. When they are officiating, the assistant referees often know when their opposite number will need to make a decision. For example, in a split second, they might need to decide whether an attacking player is offside. The laws of Association football state that an attacker can only be offside if the ball is played forward by one of their teammates. Occasionally, assistant referees make wrong decisions because they cannot see the ball being deflected by a defender. In reality, the person making the decision may not have the line of sight. However, it is possible that their fellow assistant referee might. Howard Webb explained that his assistant referees know these moments. They are aware of the information that their teammate needs and when they need it.

Gold-medal-winning Olympic coach Chris Bartle often talks about the importance of 'the system'. In equestrian sports, this system is the fundamental mechanism through which the rider and horse communicate with each other. As you can imagine, there's not a lot of verbal communication between horse and rider. The rider communicates with the horse primarily through their movements. It is vital that both the horse and the rider understand the same thing. Messages need to be simple and clear. If there is a difference in the interpretation of a movement (that is, the horse and rider understand something differently in any given movement), the performance will be compromised. Ultimately, the system is critically important to their success in competition.

It is because everyone knows exactly what a glance, wink or nod of the head means that these simple signals provide a powerful communication system. SAS major Floyd Woodrow emphasised that during operations behind enemy lines, there are many occasions where silence is normal. Importantly, each person knows what the hand signals and subtle glances mean. Because they understand these things in the same way, communication is highly effective. Of course, this doesn't happen by accident. Practise is the vital ingredient. As Andy Beadsworth also explains, it only happens when teammates are focused on each other and aware of each other. He knows where the pressure is likely to build, so he looks for it. As the leader, he deliberately looks to take cues from certain individuals at specific times.

This is another simple, but vital, element of teamwork. In my research into world-class teams I was fortunate to study a rock band, The Boxer Rebellion, at work. I asked the band how they manage to coordinate their timing on stage. Drummer Piers Hewitt told me, 'It starts with me, the drummer, but can change with the song. I make sure that everyone is ready and then lead everyone in. On a badly lit stage this can be a problem, but ultimately by focusing on me, they know when they need to pick up.'

The messages we use must be meaningful

In order to create this telepathic understanding, we need to know each other. We need to ensure that our messages are simple and clear. We need to ensure that we understand the same thing in any given message. We need to be cued into each other. We need to know what to look for and listen for. Of course, as basketball coach Phil Jackson recognises, in order to do this we have to be more interested in the team than we are in ourselves.[3]

When is a conversation not a conversation?

What actually happens during a conversation? Theory suggests that we take it in turns to talk and to listen. When somebody else is talking, we listen, then we respond to what they're saying and add to the dialogue. In a group, we all do this to progress the conversation. It is a fine theory, but how often does that actually happen in practice? As you will have noticed, in order to truly respond to what the other people in the conversation are saying, we need to actively listen.

So, what actually happens in practice?

In reality, I suspect that a number of things happen in a conversation. Rather than actively listening while someone else is speaking, we might start to formulate our response. Instead of being fully focused on their words, we start to think about our own words. We become more engaged in the conversation

▶

inside our own minds as we rehearse and play out the response before delivering it. The problem, of course, is that in doing so we are unable to truly listen to the other person.

I would also suggest that there is a second process that takes us away from really listening to the content of the conversation. Rather than actively listening to what they're saying, we listen for a gap in the conversation. We're trying to find the pause so that we can inject our response. I suspect that we listen to the tone and pattern of the conversation to detect that point at which we can interject but maybe not to the words or the meaning.

If that is how we hold conversations, we're unlikely to become world-class communicators.

Floyd Woodrow knows that leading SAS units into battle is demanding. As the leader, he relies on a foundation of trust. Arguably, developing this trust requires more than one component. Floyd explained that one of the most crucial elements is to develop an emotional connection with people. He emphasises that you have to connect with people emotionally, which comes when you really listen to them, engage with them and look them in the eye when they're talking to you. Again, it all sounds very obvious but few people do it consistently.

Communication is not always necessary

Interestingly, sometimes our ability to work together doesn't actually require any communication at all. Some world-class animal teams manage to hunt together without communicating. Biologist Dr Dan Franks explained that orca pods in the North Atlantic hunt shoals of herring by corralling them in a net of bubbles. Members of the pod dive deep, beneath the shoal, and swim around the mass of fish releasing air bubbles through their blow holes. The fish will not swim through the bubbles, so they become trapped in the net. This allows other members of the pod to stun the trapped fish with powerful slaps of their tails. The orca then feed on the stunned fish.

I asked Dan how the members of the pod know which job to do. Do the same whales do the same jobs each time? How do they allocate the roles? Researchers have discovered that the whales may allocate roles according to their experience. In other animal teams, individuals often change roles. Like many teams, they all know what needs to be done, so they simply pick up one of the roles that no one else is doing. If there are enough members of the team doing one job, others will find another role to fill in the gaps.

When I reflected on this, it is the same principle that my wife and I often adopt when we're getting the children ready for school. If she hasn't prepared the girls' snacks, I'll simply pick that up and do it. We both know what needs doing. By simply checking what has been done and what's left, we also fill in the gaps. We may or may not communicate what has been done and what hasn't. Often we'll be watching and listening to what is going on around us, but we don't explicitly discuss who is going to do the various jobs, we just get on and do what's needed. Obviously, in order to do this we need to be aware of each other and both need to have the same goal: getting the girls off to school on time with everything they need.

Design team choreography

Earlier I explained that the Lotus Formula One pit crew change all four wheels on the car in approximately 2.5 seconds. The margin for error in competition is tiny. Although a 2.5-second pit change is considered to be successful, a 3.0-second change is a disaster. The level of teamwork required to deliver their performance is astounding. To the naked eye, the whole exercise looks like a blur. How is it that the team is capable of coordinating the movements of all 16 race engineers so precisely?

Looking at the pit change more closely, it is possible to see that although the team's job is complex, each member of the team has a very simple and clearly defined role. Each car has four wheels, which are referred to as the 'corners'. At each corner, there are three engineers. One is the gunman: his responsibility is to unscrew the nut (which holds the wheel on) and then tighten it once the wheel has been changed. The second engineer in each corner is the wheel-off man: his job, very simply, is to remove the wheel. The third person is known as the wheel-on man: you don't need me to tell you what his job is, I'm sure. At the front of the box is the front jack man, who inserts the jack under the nose of the car. At the rear, there is the rear jack man. On the centre left of the box is an engineer who steadies the car while it is in the air. Finally, there is the race team manager who oversees the entire operation and releases the car when he sees the four green lights that indicate the wheels have been correctly fitted.

Everyone in the team is crucial to success.

Importantly, each pit-crew member has a very simple job. That does not mean that it is easy to do! The gunman, in particular, needs to focus his attention fully on the wheel and the nut as the car comes into the pit. He needs to engage the gun onto the nut as soon as possible and apply the trigger so that the gun unscrews the nut on the wheel. A delay of even 0.1 seconds is huge in a Formula One pit change. As the nut is loosened, the gunman rocks backwards and clears the way for the wheel-off man to remove the wheel. The wheel-off man listens to the sound of the hydraulic gun (which is pretty loud) and coordinates his movement with the release of the trigger. As the nut is unscrewed and the pressure on the wheel is released, the wheel-off man responds by removing the wheel in a clean, sweeping motion. Believe me, it sounds easier than it is! As the wheel comes off, the wheel-on man watches for the gap to appear between the wheel and the car as it is removed. As that chink of daylight appears, the wheel-on man puts the new wheel in place. It is a skilled movement, and one that takes a great deal of practice. It's very easy to lose vital fractions of a second by bumping the wheel as it goes on. Finally, the gunman watches the motion of the new wheel as it goes on. He follows the wheel in so that he can connect with the nut and pull the trigger to tighten it at the earliest possible moment. If the engineers in the pit crew are not focused on these cues, they will lose time through each of these interactions. Slippages of 0.1 seconds on each of these stages can add up to almost 0.5 seconds: the difference between success and failure.

This level of coordination is possible because everyone has a very simple and clearly defined role. They also know what cues to look for and listen to, whether it is the sound of the gun or the movement of the wheel. When they see, hear or feel their cue, they execute their task. When everyone does this, the team works.

Former National Football League coach Jeff Reinebold commented on the simple foundations that have underpinned many years of success at the New England Patriots. He explained that coach Bill Belichick starts by ensuring that everyone knows their job and is held accountable for delivering it.

The Red Arrows team works in a very similar way. Their displays are made up of a number of moves, which the team have practised relentlessly. During the display, the leader, Red One, issues the commands to specific pilots or to the team as a whole. These commands dictate the timing of the moves. Pilots know which move to expect, so instructions such as 'smoke, on, go' simply synchronise the actions of each individual. In order to keep their place in the formation, each pilot also takes cues from the other aeroplanes around them. They know the distance and angles that they need to maintain, in order to fly as part of the team. It all comes down to focusing on the right cues, at the right time.

Understand how interdependencies work

As the Lotus Formula One pit crew will testify, great teams understand that the members are dependent upon each other. They are acutely aware of how their actions affect the performance of their teammates and ultimately the success of the team. Importantly, they don't just understand that their actions affect others, but they also know *how*. I often help teams to understand the interdependency that exists. It starts with the recognition that 'I need you to do X, so that I can do Y, and we can deliver Z.' Although this sounds incredibly obvious, I have found very few team members who actually understand how they impact upon each other's performance.

A little while ago I worked with a recruitment consultancy. Unwittingly, the members of the team were causing problems for their teammates because they were so focused on doing their own job that they forgot about the job of the team. In particular, the recruitment consultants were focused on delivering their key performance indicators (KPIs) and fees. The inconvenient little jobs, such as the admin tasks, were often relegated to the back burner. Although that seemed to liberate the recruitment consultants to focus on the fees, it had a detrimental impact on the business as a whole. Lack of admin meant that the business leaders didn't have the management information required to make critical business decisions. When the admin fell behind, the management didn't truly have their finger on the pulse of the business. Therefore, important decisions on how to manage the cash flow were being made on inaccurate or outdated information. When the consultants understood how their actions affected the team as a whole, the importance of admin tasks became apparent. Teams tend to perform much better when people understand not just why they need to do their bit for others but also why they need to do it *well*.

What impact do teammates have on each other?

When I see teams at work, I am interested to know how team members impact on each other's performance. Do they inhibit each other's performance and have a negative impact? Do they allow each other to perform (a neutral impact)? Or, do they enable each other to perform and have a positive impact? Although it might sound strange, even in sports that are apparently individual, such as swimming teams and track-and-field teams, teammates can influence each other's performance. Aside from the obvious examples of relay teams, there is often an environment within the team that either helps each athlete to perform or interferes. In the better teams, athletes know that they have an opportunity to coach each other, advise each other, offer critical and constructive feedback, push each other and relay useful information or experiences. They are also able to generate positive energy by choosing to contribute positively to the environment rather than moan and blame others.

FIFA World Cup referee Howard Webb echoed this sentiment. In his experience, refereeing in front of 80,000 people can be intimidating, especially when you're making unpopular decisions. When 80,000 people think you're wrong, you know about it! Howard says, 'Having radio links between us all is the single biggest change that I've experienced in my refereeing career. Having your mates in your ears is vital. You need the balances, checks and measures from a credible, impartial source. They provide emotional support, but also help you focus on the right information and provide reliable information. I lost radio contact for the first 20 minutes of a World Cup game in Brazil recently. It felt like I'd lost two pairs of eyes and ears.'

One way that I briefly assess whether teammates are inhibiting, allowing or enabling each other's performance is to listen to their conversations. Do the conversations build on the input and contributions that each person makes? Are they actually listening to each other and looking for ways to enhance the dialogue? Or are they more concerned with their own response and looking for the pause in the discussion to make their point, as I discussed earlier? If we have a clear, strong and shared purpose, and we all understand the job simply and clearly, there is a very good chance that we'll actively do things that enable each other to perform better. In the absence of these things, we're likely to put our own priorities ahead of other people's and focus on advancing our own agenda.

Pinpoint the interdependencies

To help a team understand the interdependencies and the way in which they impact each other's performance, I often ask team members to fill in the blanks for the following statements:

- 'At the moment I get frustrated when ...'

- 'My life can be made more difficult if ...'

- 'We would definitely step up a gear if we just ...'

- 'To do my job better, it would really help if ...'

- 'If I could make a request of someone, I would ask ...'

- 'I think I could help someone else by ...'

- 'I can see an opportunity for us to be more effective if we ...'

- 'We'd be a great team if we consistently ...'

How creativity can be collective

Most organisations understand the importance of innovating and developing new solutions to problems. Some go further and appreciate the need to be creative. Therefore, being able to work together to deliver creative solutions can be incredibly valuable. Rock drummer Piers Hewitt explained how his band, The Boxer Rebellion, co-creates music. Interestingly, the band also has its own record label. The label that they originally signed with imploded as the band launched their first album. Since that time, they have been working together as a business as well as a musical quartet. They book their own gigs, arrange the travel, promote their own albums and even sell the merchandise. They are used to solving problems together. In Piers's words, they are a true partnership. Everyone understands that they need to deliver their individual roles, both on and off the stage, so that the band can perform. This philosophy also translates to writing new material, as Piers explained:

> The process has evolved during the years. We split royalties four ways equally, no matter how the song comes about or how it is created. No one focuses on their own agenda. We bring our own skills and appreciate each other's skills. If one person really doesn't like something, they have the right to veto.
>
> We throw out three times as much [material] as we keep, easily. We're all happy throwing material away. No one takes it personally if we throw their ideas or

contributions out. It's a pretty democratic system. We're one of the most equal bands that I know. No one is bigger than the team; we have no superstars. If someone gets too big for their boots, we'll tell them. Everyone pulls together.

Why effective teams are essential in crisis situations

As I'm sure you know, it's easier for a team to be synchronised when things are going well, but what happens when the conditions change? What happens when teams find themselves in crisis situations? How do great teams respond when the smelly stuff hits the fan?

In medicine there is an infamous case that highlighted the need for surgical teams to work together more effectively. On 29 March 2005, Elaine Bromiley died during routine surgery. Kevin Fong – a consultant anaesthetist at University College London Hospitals and the Anaesthetic Lead for both the Patient Emergency Response Team and Major Incident Planning – investigated the case for a BBC *Horizon* documentary.[4] In the programme he explains, 'The weakest link is not the drugs or equipment, it is us; the surgical team.' Elaine Bromiley was admitted to surgery for a routine sinus operation in a private clinic. There was nothing out of the ordinary as the team prepared the patient for the procedure. During a process known as intubation, a tube is placed in the patient's throat, which keeps the airway open and allows them to breathe. Out of the blue, a severe problem arose. Elaine's airway became blocked and the anaesthetist could not insert the tube. A second anaesthetist was called, along with an ear, nose and throat specialist, but to no avail. Twenty-five minutes passed and the situation became critical. Starved of oxygen, Elaine Bromiley slipped into a coma and died 13 days later.

Incredibly, there was a tracheotomy kit available, but it wasn't used. The report into the Elaine Bromiley case stated that it was not clear who was in charge during the emergency. A nurse also offered the tracheotomy kit but was ignored by the more senior doctors. Although the nurse knew the tracheotomy kit could be life-saving, he felt unable to broach the solution forcefully enough to the doctors. Clearly, the team didn't work.

Under pressure, the team's decision-making became fatally compromised. Fortunately, this event triggered a radical change in the way surgical teams work. Simple checklists, like those used in aviation, now enable team members to follow essential processes and coordinate their actions in critical situations. This allows everyone to know their job and how they relate to their teammates. Interestingly, Dr Alan Goldman, a specialist in human factors within medicine, found that teams using check-lists during the handover process between surgery and the ward reduced human errors by 40 per cent.[5] Perhaps more impor-tantly, it reduces the incidence of small errors that could potentially compound and become major incidents. In the words of Dr Goldman, 'The little things start going wrong, which leads to error cascading and then the big things go wrong.'

Crises unpack in seconds

A similar approach is adopted within civil aviation. On 15 January 2009, the world watched as US Airways Flight 1549 hit a flock of birds moments after take-off from LaGuardia Airport in New York. Both engines were hit and the aeroplane immediately lost thrust. Captain Chesley Sullenberger was at the controls. He said, 'Both engines were gone all at once.' It was something that Captain Sullenberger had never experienced before and a sce-nario that he'd never specifically trained for. 'I felt my peripheral field narrow … The plane became a clumsy glider.'[6] Captain Sullenberger explained that his first response was fear, followed immediately by implementing procedures that he had practised for years. With the sound of the alarms ringing in their ears, Captain Sullenberger and his co-pilot, Jeffrey Skiles, began monitoring their systems and liaising with Air Traffic Control. They tried to reignite the engines, but it quickly became apparent that both engines were dead. They then worked through a series of possible emergency landing options, including a return to LaGuardia or a right turn to Teterboro airfield in New Jersey. These were also quickly negated as the plane lost power. All this happened in a little over a minute. The transcript from the flight recorder shows that 60.2 seconds after the bird strike, Captain Sullenberger says, 'We're unable. We may end up in the Hudson.' After reviewing options further, Captain Sullenberger confirms his intentions, 'We're gonna be in the Hudson.' He instructs the passengers to brace. Then he and First Officer Skiles ran through their landing sequence: 'Got flaps out ... Two hundred fifty feet in the air ... Hundred and seventy knots ... Got flaps two, you want more? ... No let's stay at two ... Brace.'

Incredibly, not one of the 155 passengers or crew were killed or seriously injured when US Airways flight 1549 ditched in the Hudson River. In his accounts after the event, Captain Sullenberger explained that it was possible because he had confidence in his training; 'If I can put the plane flat on the surface it'll float OK.'

Great teams in critical moments

In many cases, the way in which world-class teams operate in critical moments differentiates them from the rest. Some have normal ways of functioning and communicating that are robust enough to withstand dramatic changes in circumstance. Others have planned and practised their response to the 'what ifs?'. Organisations such as NASA appear to have developed systems that are designed specifically to operate in critical moments.

Space is perhaps the most hostile environment that we know. Astronauts operating in the International Space Station (ISS), 250 miles above the earth, are acutely aware of just how vulnerable they are. This is exacerbated during EVAs (space walks), where things can go from calm and controlled to life-threatening in moments.

On 11 December 2013 an emergency warning flashed on the monitors at Mission Control in Houston. One of the two cooling units on the ISS had failed. If the second cooling unit failed as well, those aboard the ISS would be placed in a life-threatening situation. Immediately, analyst Scott Stover looked at the potential consequences. Mission Control decided to attempt to reboot the cooling units automatically from Houston and also manually from within the ISS. However, both attempts failed.

NASA knows that the primary responsibility is to keep people alive, so all non-essential operations on the ISS were shut down. Nevertheless, they were just one step away from evacuating the space station.

Aboard the ISS the astronauts prepared the space suits for an emergency EVA to repair the cooling unit. Interestingly, just five months earlier on the previous space walk, one of the helmets filled with water and almost drowned European Space Agency (ESA) astronaut Luca Palmitano. Although the suits had been modified, they had not been tested in space since.

NASA senior management held a crisis meeting to find a solution. Team Four were tasked with planning the EVA. This involved a full underwater simulation, in space suits, on a full-sized replica section of the ISS, held in the world's largest indoor swimming pool – the Neutral Buoyancy Lab in Houston – on 17 December. Data from the simulation was then processed and sent to the astronauts on the ISS. Hundreds of people were involved in preparing an EVA that would be executed by just two astronauts.

A NASA flight director said, 'Five days later, not only have we come up with a solution, but we've rehearsed it in the water, rehearsed it in the high-fidelity mock up and walked the crew [on the ISS] through it a few times.'

During the mission, all the communication to and from the astronauts was conducted by one person, known as the capsule communicator (CAPCOM). This simple process ensures that there are not too many voices and that communication is 'clean'. Through CAPCOM, problems were relayed from the astronauts to the team in Houston, solutions were found and passed back to the astronauts.

As Mike Massimino, NASA astronaut and mission specialist, says, 'You're never alone up there.'

Missions such as these highlight the incredible levels of teamwork that are required to fix a cooling unit on an object travelling at 17,500kmph, in a vacuum, in micro-gravity, 250 miles above the surface of the earth.

World-class communication

The above mission shows how NASA has created incredibly clear lines of communication. There is only one person at Mission Control who talks to the astronauts during an EVA. That person is the CAPCOM. When critical decisions are required, they are passed to the flight director. In addition to the immediate team around the flight director, there are a number of other specialist teams. These teams, such as Team Four, will be engaged to solve specific problems. Importantly, NASA has developed a simple and effective line of communication to get a problem to the right team, and a solution back to the astronauts, quickly.

Communication in the Red Arrows is also streamlined and highly effective. Like many other teams in military aviation, the Red Arrows understand that effective communication has a number of key qualities. During an operation, pilots only speak when there is something important to say. If there is nothing important to say, they keep quiet. Every communication is relevant, accurate, timely, concise and well directed.

They understand the *who?*, *what?*, *why?*, *when?* and *how?* of communication:

- Why is this important?

- What do I need to say?

- Who do I need to get this message to?

- How can I best communicate it?

- When do they need to know?

Of course, this is very different from the pattern that many people use:

- I want to say something.

- I need to get something off my chest.

- I am going to let them know what I think.

- I'll tell them what I think in an email and copy everyone else in – that'll show them.

- I don't care when it's good for them, I'm saying it now.

Of course, world-class communication does not happen by chance. FIFA World Cup referee Howard Webb explained that their pre-match briefings focus specifically on how they will communicate: 'We clarify the exact words that we will use, what information we need and when we need it.'

Interestingly, NASA's CAPCOM, Doug Wheelock, quoted this from Fellini: 'If there were just a little more silence ... if we all kept quiet ... maybe we could finally understand ...'

Thriving in chaos

It is possible to develop a team's ability to respond to sudden changes in circumstance. James Kerr describes how the All Blacks rugby team do this by continually exposing the team to uncertainty and change.[7] The coaching staff deliberately engineer challenges that force the team to solve problems collectively. It enables the team to become better at encountering challenges and unknown situations together. They begin to understand how each other operates and how to collaborate and create high-quality solutions together.

Tom Peters, author of *Thriving On Chaos*, proposes that to be able to thrive on chaos, we need highly skilled and adaptable experts, with a broad base of knowledge and experience.[8] This broad base of experience provides a greater level of adaptability by allowing people to transfer experiences in one realm to another. It is something that Tom Peters sees in genuine craftsmen. In his view, hyper-specialism creates rigidity in people and makes it difficult for people to re-specialise and develop new skills. In sports, many teams now aim to develop players that have a wide skills base and who can play in multiple positions. Modern-day rugby union forwards need to be able to have the ball skills and running skills of the backs. Equally, the backs need to be able to ruck and tackle like the forwards.

I've been working with a number of elite professional sports teams to help them to weave 'chaos training' into their practice sessions. The aim, very simply, is to ask questions and pose challenges that the team need to answer collectively. These challenges instil specific skills within the team. In sport there is a basic pattern. First, we need to recognise that there is a change we need to respond to. Sometimes the signals can be pretty subtle, so we all need to know what we're looking and listening for. Once we have detected the need to change, we need to use our collective knowledge and experience to formulate a response. It's likely that in the heat of competition we're not going to have time to debate the issue in depth. Often there are one or two leaders in the team who initiate the change. Sometimes this will be communicated verbally. Sometimes it won't. In many cases the rest of the team need to be aware of the leaders – to watch their moves and to follow. We also know that our first plan may not provide the complete solution. We might need to refine the plan and go again, or change tack. Obviously, the success of this approach depends upon the entire team being aware of each other's movements and actions.

How does this apply to you?

This simple methodology can also be applied to business teams every day. It's not rocket science. In my work with executive leadership teams, we develop the team's ability to collectively solve problems by ... collectively solving problems.

Summary

World-class teams have a compelling reason to exist. There is also a strong rationale for team members to invest in each other. We don't have to be in the middle of a war zone to develop super-strong bonds, but we do have to remember how human relationships are built. For teams to work, we have to be focused on each other and know which cues to be tuned into. We can develop synchronicity by understanding how we respond to changes in our environment; when X happens, I need to do Y. Understanding how we're interdependent also helps us to enable our teammates to perform, instead of inhibiting them. All these things can be developed when we spend time collectively solving problems.

- Understand why you need a team to exist and give it a clear rationale.

- A deep understanding of each other in the team is fundamental to effective teamwork. Take the necessary time to invest in your relationships by getting to know each other thoroughly.

- Build trust and respect, and a bank of gratitude with each other, to strengthen the bond and reinforce the team.

- Build synchronicity by creating a common understanding. Be able to rethink collectively when unexpected urgent action is required.

- Develop ways to engineer-out the need for verbal communication by understanding things in the same way.

- Understand the *why?, what?, how?, who?* and *when?* of communication.

- Be familiar with each other's roles and have shared signals. Learn how to connect with people fully by really listening to them and engaging with them.

- Work together for maximum efficiency by choreographing movements, jobs and roles.

- Make sure that every team member understands the aims of the whole team or organisation – to put their role into perspective and to highlight the interdependencies.

- Effective teams are essential in crisis situations. When we understand how to deal with something unexpected and serious we increase the likelihood of a positive outcome. To prepare, factor in challenges – chaos training – to force the team to solve problems collectively.

WORKSHOP: World-class teamwork

Take a moment to reflect on what you see in your team at the moment. Score your team using the simple 0–10 scale. As before, a score of 10 means 'perfect, flawless, cannot be improved'. A score of zero means that there is nothing good about it.

How well do you:

1   Understand the need to work together as a team?
2   Collectively respond to changes in your environment?
3   Recognise interdependencies?
4   Ensure that everyone knows their job and is held accountable for delivery?
5   Adopt 'less is more' communication?
6   Collectively solve problems?

What can you do to improve your score for each by just one? See 'What Can You Learn?' on page 12 and use the summary above to suggest ways that you can improve the way your team players work together.

CHAPTER 5

Improving Team Performance

How can we turn around an under-performing team? What do great leaders do to turn the tide and get their team heading in the right direction? How do sports coaches get their team firing on all cylinders again? Equally, how can we take a good team and enable it to be great, or even a great team and help it to become world class?

If you believe what you see in the movies, you might think that great leaders do this by delivering an epic speech. Whether it is the battle cry of William Wallace in *Braveheart,* the half-time pep-talk from coach Tony D'Amato in *Any Given Sunday*, The president's speech in *Independence Day*, or one of the many 'get back in there and fight' pep-talks from *Rocky*, we could get fooled into thinking that only great orators can turn their team around. In my experience, the truth is very different.

Identify the reason to improve

Although epic pep-talks in themselves may not boost performance, in the film *Any Given Sunday*, the famous 'inches' speech given by coach Tony D'Amato (played by Al Pacino) did emphasise why the team needed to improve: 'Either we heal now, as a team, or we will die, as individuals.'

It sounds rather obvious, but any team needs a strong reason to improve. Getting better requires effort. It demands more from us. We need to think more, ask ourselves tougher questions and invest more of ourselves. Improving isn't comfortable. Therefore, human beings often need a strong reason to do it. I recently spoke to a senior executive in a global corporation. His team was already very good. In fact, recently, it had become the number-one brand in their industry. To his dismay, his team began to ease off when they surpassed their competition and became the market leader. Before they hit the front, the team had a strong reason to become better. Collectively, they wanted to be 'number one'. As soon as they achieved that goal, the reason to get better evaporated. Why should they now invest the time and effort to become better still?

New Zealand's national rugby team, the All Blacks, completed 2013 with an incredible 100 per cent winning record. They began the year as the world's number-one team, having won 12, drawn 1 and lost just 1 of their 14 matches in 2012. Interestingly, after a convincing 47–29 victory against the Wallabies in Australia during their first Rugby Championship match of 2013, the All Blacks' coach, Steve Hanson, said they needed to get 15 per cent better in every game. Steve Hanson and the All Blacks know that you cannot rely on the opposition under-performing, so you need to continually look for ways to improve your own performance. Becoming the number-one team might be tough, but arguably it's even more difficult to maintain pole position. When there is no one to chase, and no one blueprint to follow, you have to look at your own game and work out where to find the next few per cent.

The reasons to improve tend to be more obvious when teams are in crisis. However, many teams genuinely understand the need to constantly improve even when they are doing well. In some highly successful cultures, winning has become the norm. Therefore, the thought of losing drives them to seek out ways to get better. In most walks of life, standing still equates to going backwards. In fact, moving forwards more slowly than those around you also equates to going backwards. If we recognise that we're in a competitive world, those who are going backwards don't tend to be around for very long. For most of us, survival is the reason to improve. The only reason that we're not acutely aware of this on a moment-by-moment basis is that failing to improve can be a slow death. Sometimes we may not even realise that the reason we're dying is because we're not getting better fast enough.

The magic one minute

While working in the English Premier League a few years ago, I sometimes found it tough to engage the players in training exercises. I managed to get some of the players to engage some of the time, but I couldn't seem to get all of them all the time. I reflected on this during the off-season period. I decided to make a very subtle change in the way I delivered sessions at the beginning of the next pre-season. I introduced the 'magic one minute', as I call it. At the beginning of the session I would take a minute to explain exactly why we were doing the exercise and how it would benefit our performance on the field. On one occasion I explained that the session was specifically designed to help us to avoid conceding goals in the last five minutes of a game. During the previous year I had seen the team concede late goals that cost us dearly. With this simple understanding, the players had a reason to engage in the session. If I saw the focus drop, I would ask whether it was important for us to work on our performance in the last five minutes, or not? Was it worth investing a bit of focus, energy and attention to this, or not?

▶

> The difference in engagement was significant. During the previous season, I had assumed that the players would know the purpose of the session. However, it soon became obvious that they didn't. Once I took time to explain why we were doing each session, the players had a much more compelling reason to invest themselves in it.

Watch out for the danger zones

There is, of course, a close relationship between our processes and the outcomes that result. In many cases, there is a lag phase between delivering better processes and seeing the improved results. The length of this delay will be different from one environment to the next. In some cases, changes in our processes may translate to results in a few days. In other cases, we may not see the impact on results for weeks or months. Of course, the sensitivity of our measures will often dictate how quickly we notice the progress. If we measured a swimmer's progress in whole seconds, he could get half a second quicker (which is a massive gain in elite swimming) and conclude that he's not improving. Only by measuring in hundredths or even thousandths of a second will we start to see the first signs of progress emerging.

It's also common to see two danger zones. The first appears when people are experiencing the delay between improving their processes and the change in results. Improving our processes usually requires greater effort and demands more from us. If we haven't seen the corresponding up-turn in the results, we may end up becoming despondent, concluding that all this extra effort is wasted. Why bother investing the energy if the results don't follow?

The second danger zone appears at the top of the curve, when the increase in results has been realised. Knowing that there is a delay between improving our processes and seeing results, it stands to reason that the opposite is also true. If we start to take our foot off the gas when the results are good, we might not notice the drop in results immediately. Inevitably though, if we reduce the quality of the processes, the results will follow; it is just a matter of time. At the top of the curve, therefore, many people become complacent. They opt to take it easy when the results are good, forgetting that the outcomes will follow the processes.

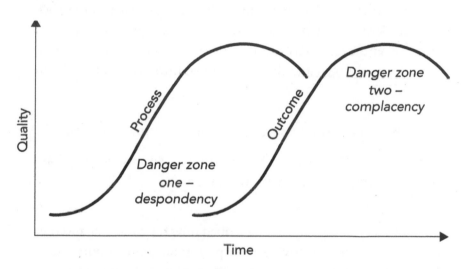

The relationship between processes and results

The trick is not to depend on the increase in results but to continually focus on improving the processes for their own sake.

Improving is a constant – it's an 'all-the-time thing'

Some people could feel threatened when they're asked how they can improve their performance. Is the question being asked because my performance is not good enough? Is this part of the disciplinary process? Am I being performance managed? Am I failing and is this just a way of dressing up the message?

The All Blacks are a great example of a team that makes constant improvement a habit. They don't just ask how they can get better when the results start to slide. World-class organisations don't tend to hold impromptu team meetings to get things back on track once they have derailed. Conversations about the need to become ever better are part of the day-to-day discussions. They are expected and therefore woven into their cultural landscape:

Q: Why are we discussing performance improvement today?

A: Because the sun rose this morning ... Because the day has a 'y' in it ... Because it's what we always do!

Yacht skipper Brendan Hall described how his crew became completely engaged in driving their performance.[1] Of course, they wanted to win the race, so it was their collective aim to make the boat sail as fast as possible. They all thought about how to make their boat go quicker. Everyone chipped in with ideas about how to reduce the weight of the boat so that they could increase the speed. They decided to have 'community shampoo', to avoid having 20 individual bottles on board. Although it might only have saved a few grams, it illustrated that the team were all focused on improving their performance.

When improvements are part of our everyday conversation, we find ourselves actively looking for ways to get better. When we're looking for ways to improve, we tend to find the opportunities. Much of my focus, when working with teams, is spent helping them understand how their reviews, planning, preparation, practice and performance all underpin results. Which processes do we need to focus on? How good is our game plan? How well do we execute it? On a scale of 0–10 (if 10 represents 'perfect, flawless and cannot be improved'), where are we right now? What could we do to become just one point better? What can we do to enhance our reviews, planning, preparation, practice and therefore our performance?

Over time, I have noticed that more and more of the team become actively engaged in this process. They begin to look for opportunities without being prompted. Conversations begin to spark more spontaneously and not only in the presence of the leaders. It actually becomes a common way of thinking! People begin to understand that improving performance actually tends to make their life easier and gives them greater satisfaction. Therefore, they are happy to find ways to build on an eight out of ten performance and push it towards a nine.

The nuts and bolts

Teams are made up of people. Therefore, it stands to reason that increasing team performance requires us to increase the performance of the individuals. Experience tells me that human beings tend to perform well when they are focused, confident and motivated. These basic ingredients give us the psychological foundation to perform. I have also found that to perform well in any given task, we normally need to have the knowledge, skills, resources and desire to do it. Therefore, if I see somebody struggling, I normally take time to see whether these are present, or whether some are missing. Of course, resources can be provided, knowledge can be learned and skills developed, if the desire is there. Red Arrows team leader Jas Hawker outlined a very simple process that they use to assess whether a person's performance is likely to improve and how much energy to invest in them.

- If a person has **neither the capability nor attitude**, they're probably a lost cause and not worth investing in.

- If a person has the **capability but a poor attitude**, they may be worth a measured amount of investment but could end up becoming a lost cause.

- If a person has a **great attitude but is low on capability**, it's worth investing in them and tracking their progress closely.

- If a person has a **great attitude and the capability**, you tend not to have any issues.

Attitude is, of course, the critical component.

In my book *Two Lengths of the Pool*, I describe a very simple mechanism for helping people to consistently perform at their best. To perform well, we need to be focused on the right thing at the right time. Therefore, it all starts by honing our focus and understanding our 'two lengths of the pool' – our job in the simplest possible terms.[2] When Olympic swimmer Chris Cook realised that his job was simply to swim two lengths of the pool as quickly as he could, he became very good at doing it. That formula doesn't just apply to Chris. When we understand our job, we also stand a very good chance of performing well. What are the key processes that we need to focus on to do that job?

In addition to knowing that his job was to swim two lengths of the pool as quickly as he could, Chris also identified his 'five keys': the top five things that would allow him to do this. As a very professional and diligent athlete, Chris had previously tried to do everything possible. If you asked him to write a list of things that he could do to swim quicker, there would have been several hundred things on his list. The problem, of course, is that humans can't do hundreds of things well. We need a tight focus.

It is not just Chris who understood his job with this level of clarity. In his book, *Winning!*, Sir Clive Woodward identifies five key elements for each rugby player's role in the team.[3] In *Team Spirit*, skipper Brendan Hall also identified five key elements that were crucial to making the boat go as fast as possible:

1 Crew management

2 Integrating the leggers [see page 90] into the crew as smoothly and quickly as possible

3 Keeping up morale and a sense of fun

4 Effective conflict management

5 Create a culture of knowledge sharing, openness and team solidarity – a great place to be[4]

The crew of *Spirit of Australia* also made sure that every brief, for every manoeuvre on the boat, allowed each crew member to know exactly what they needed to do. Simplicity and clarity of focus are the foundation.

Confidence comes through focus

A simple, clear focus actually helps us to become confident. When we have a clear focus, and execute our processes well, we become confident. And, when we're confident in our performance we tend to want to do it again. Therefore, we also become more motivated. In order to draw confidence from our performances, we also need to ensure that we're evaluating our performances honestly and objectively, rather than judging ourselves on our results. In my post-competition conversations with athletes, they will normally kick off by telling me about their results. However, I ask them two questions: (1) How good was your game plan? and (2) How well did you execute it? In answering these questions, the athlete begins to evaluate their performance. The conversation also allows us to look at the effectiveness of their previous review and the quality of their planning, preparation and practice. By working on these things, we can begin to engineer a better performance next time.

In order to engage in this process, the person has to be interested in the performance and not just the results. It is tough for people to focus on the processes if they perceive that their success or failure hinges on the result. People who need the results in order to feel successful can take their eye off the processes and become consumed by the outcome. When this happens, they can begin to feel pressure. Feeling pressure normally changes our mental and emotional state. When athletes feel pressure, they tend not to focus on the right things at the right time and will consequently make mistakes. If they perceive that mistakes are bad they could also begin to try too hard, think too much and then make a bigger mistake. It doesn't take long for the performance to deteriorate. As they try ever harder to engineer the outcome they want, it ends up drifting further away. Therefore, the start point in helping turn around a performance is often to become more interested in the processes and to focus on them completely.

The same is true collectively. How can we hone our focus so that it becomes simple and clear? What is our 'two lengths of the pool' as a team – our job in the simplest possible terms? Which key processes do we need to focus on and execute well? How good was our game plan? How well did we execute it? How can we review, plan, prepare and practise better? Of course, in order for 'us' to make improvements, all the individuals have to think differently and do things differently.

Briefings bring clarity

The military are famed for their rigorous use of briefings. The aim of the briefing is very simple: it is a way of ensuring that everyone knows exactly what they're supposed to do before they get started. It sits between planning and execution normally, and serves to help us deliver the plan. Organisations such as the SAS, the Red Arrows and NASA deliver some of the best briefings in the world. It is a necessity for them because the margin for error is minute. They will walk through manoeuvres and the 'what ifs?' over and over again to make sure that everyone is completely ready to go. Before each display, the Red Arrows will sit in the briefing room and run through all the calls from each of the pilots, in the order that they will happen. It is like actors rehearsing their lines before stepping onto the stage. Once the plans have been constructed at Mission Control in Houston, NASA teams will complete several walk-throughs of an EVA (spacewalk) before the astronauts put their spacesuits on and step out into the vacuum of space.

In many cases, the briefings have multiple layers. Skipper Brendan Hall explained the multiple levels of briefing that he used aboard *Spirit of Australia*.[5] There was a major briefing before the race and before the start of each leg. Here they would outline the challenges that they were likely to encounter and the plans that were in place to overcome them. As the skipper, Brendan also knew that the flow of information was crucial to maintain confidence and morale on the boat, so every day they also had a lunchtime briefing during the race. He took time to explain decisions, changes to planning and why they had been made. They also briefed before each manoeuvre to ensure that everyone knew exactly what they were doing. In Brendan's words, 'It removes uncertainty and anxiety when everyone knows what the plan is and they know their role.'

Simplicity and clarity underpin confidence ... and confidence underpins motivation.

Raising the bar

Raising the bar does not simply mean increasing the target! I'm sure you have seen managers who think that adding 20 per cent to the sales target is a way of raising the bar. Equally, sports coaches that walk in and tell their team that they expect to win trophies are not raising the bar either. I recently had a conversation with a client who runs a very successful business. He told me that he wasn't willing to lower his expectations, because standards were critically important. In response I said, 'These two words mean very different things. When we talk of standards, we're referring to the quality of delivery and how well things are done. Expectations relate to a level of performance, or result, that we expect from ourselves and others. Expectations are a projection, a product of our imagination. I would argue, "So what if you expect £15k per month from each of your consultants?" Your expectation will not make the consultants any more likely to deliver the target. The most likely outcome is stress for everyone.'

Many great leaders raise the bar by increasing the challenge. They also demand ever-higher standards and greater quality. Importantly, they match this with an increase in support. In doing so, they ensure that they develop their team to deliver against the new challenge and hit the new standards. American researcher Nevitt Sanford found that people learned and developed most quickly when there was a proportional increase in support with the challenge.[6] He proposed that the greatest developments occurred when challenges increased steadily rather than suddenly. He also recognised that raising the level of challenge inevitably leads to failures. The support does not alleviate the failures, and nor should it. By providing support through the process, people learn and progress through the failures.

Do we go through adversity, or grow through adversity?

Although the sink-or-swim approach might work for some people, there is a good chance that you'll lose a lot of people along the way. Some organisations can afford to do this. In his book, *The Gold Mine Effect*, Rasmus Ankersen explains some of the reasons why Kenya is able to continually produce world-class distance runners, Jamaica can develop wave upon wave of sprinters and Brazil keeps producing world-class footballers.[7] One reason is that there are thousands of young athletes all vying to 'pass through the eye of a needle' and become a sporting great. The attrition rate is enormous. Of course, the system thrives on the basis that only a handful will make it. Therefore, the sink-or-swim approach works for them. It's different in many businesses, where staff turnover is expensive and employment laws must be adhered to. In these environments, increases in challenge and support must be carefully considered.

Change the momentum

Athletes and sports teams know the importance of controlling the psychological momentum of a contest. There is a common saying in soccer: 'goals change games'. Cricket matches are often characterised by 'batting collapses', where a team will lose three or four wickets in quick succession when a partnership is broken. If teams are not careful, the contest could swing away from them in a matter of moments. In the National Football League (NFL), turnovers tend to change, not only possession, but the dominance from one team to another. In tennis, the shifts in momentum can often be clearly visible as one player begins to gain advantage over the other. Many people would suggest that the famous comebacks in sport are prime examples of psychological momentum shifting.

Importantly, momentum shifts are not limited to sport and

often have a significant impact on performance in business. I often see the same pattern in sales people, who describe performing at their best when they're 'hot' or on a winning streak. Crucially, these examples from sport show us that shifts in momentum occur when changes in the situation impact upon how we think and feel. If a quarterback in the NFL throws an interception, he gives possession away. This could lead to a change in the score. However, it might also affect that player's decision-making and execution. If they feel that they need to atone for their error, it's possible that the quarterback then becomes more erratic and takes higher risk options. Equally, they might become more aware of making a mistake and therefore become more conservative. If they begin to think too much, they might delay a pass by a split second and miss an opportunity. Therefore, how the quarterback thinks and feels will impact on their decisions. This, in turn, will affect the game situation. Ultimately, there is a knock-on effect on the team as a whole. Changes in the game situation could affect the way the rest of the team think and feel too. Shifts in momentum occur as a result of the compound effect between changes in situation and changes in our psychology.

How does this apply to you?

Imagine that our quarterback is a sales executive who misses a few opportunities and fails to hit their target one month. It is quite possible that, in this situation, the sales executive's confidence might take a hit. I have seen sales people become 'shot shy' when their sales begin to dry up. They don't want rejections, which would further knock their confidence, so they back off. This can have a knock-on effect on the rest of the team, especially if the struggling sales executive starts to blame the economic climate, the customers, the products or the marketing.

The secret to controlling the momentum is pretty simple. In fact, that famous 'inches speech', from the film *Any Given Sunday*, provides us with the answer. In the film, the coach, Tony D'Amato, describes that, just like life, football is a game of inches. The margins between winning and losing are tiny. In football, the difference between catching the ball and missing it is half a step – or a split second. When we understand the power of this, the road to success is simple. We need to add up all those inches. We need to recognise that the opportunity to turn things around is given to us constantly, on a moment-by-moment basis. In coach D'Amato's words, 'They're in every break of the game, every minute, every second.' Rather than looking for the silver-bullet solution, we can turn things around one inch at a time. I would argue that the same principle can be applied directly to increasing profits or getting out of debt. Instead of an inch, we can do it one pound or one dollar at a time.

Controlling momentum requires us to deliver our processes really well and to take care of those small, seemingly insignificant details. If we want to turn the tide and improve our performance, we need to do it one inch at a time. It's the accumulation of those inches, not a silver-bullet solution, that helps us to regain the momentum. In sport it happens one shot at a time, one pass at a time, one tackle at a time. In soccer, if our defender gives the attacking player just 10–15cm more space, we could gift them momentum. In rugby, an attacking team might gain momentum if they cross the gain-line four times in succession, even if it is just by a few inches.

Getting the basics right is fundamentally important to success and our ability to improve our performance. It's for this reason that England's World Cup-winning rugby coach Sir Clive Woodward started his campaign by focusing on getting basic skills right.[8] It might seem bizarre when you have an international team full of experienced players. However, it's where the best coaches always seem to focus. Basketball coach John Wooden famously started his first coaching session of each season by making sure that players put their socks on properly.

In business, our decision-making and the quality of our execution, dictates whether we're gaining or losing momentum. The quality of each conversation that we have, or each meeting that we chair, or presentation that we make, could have a significant impact on momentum. Understanding this helps us to plan and prepare better. We might even decide to practise what we're going to do before we deliver it. A sales team that I worked with recently, discovered that spending an extra few minutes preparing before every phone call made a huge difference to the quality of the call and their subsequent success. They knew that 'high-impact calls' were far more likely to produce results than 'low-impact calls'. Investing an extra few seconds in preparation could dictate whether you operate with high impact or low impact.

If you want to increase performance by 10 per cent, look for a 1 per cent increase, 10 times.

If you want better answers, ask better questions

There are some teams that are almost like dormant volcanoes: waiting to erupt. They have the potential to become great, but just need a spark to ignite them. Often that spark comes in the form of a great question. A really specific and well-defined question can engage the team and give it something to sink its teeth into. Conversely, vague and ambiguous questions can lead to rambling conversations and meaningless conclusions. I have found that questions that ask a team 'How could we?' or 'How can we?' have the ability to get their collective creativity flowing. As we have seen, the Lotus Formula One pit crew have three race engineers that change each wheel of the car. This trio are known as 'the corner'. Each 'corner' is given the challenge and responsibility to ensure that they consistently change their wheel as quickly as possible. The unit have been set a question, 'How can we consistently execute the fastest wheel change possible?' The corner is given ownership over the problem. To help them answer this question, they could also ask, 'Where do we lose time? Where is there an opportunity to gain more? Where do we tend to be inconsistent? Where can we avoid losing 0.2 seconds every tenth wheel change? How do we minimise the frequency and magnitude of the outliers?'

Great questions guide our thinking. Our human brain is fantastic at solving problems. If we ask it intelligent questions, it will get to work on them and help us find possible solutions. If we ask, 'Why did we lose?' or 'Why did we fail to get that deal?', there is a very good chance that our brain will seek to find potential reasons. In doing so, we might end up with a head full of excuses. We might start to perceive that the reason we lost was due to circumstances outside our control. Therefore, there's not a lot we can do about it. With that conclusion, we'll probably not see any ways to improve our game. If, on the other hand, we ask, 'How could we have performed better and given ourselves a greater chance of winning the game?', our brain starts to answer that question. In doing so, we might see things that could be done better, or with greater consistency. We could then follow up and ask, 'What would we need to do to ensure that we are better next time?' A great question is the start point for our thought process, and directs it. Therefore, if we want great answers, it makes sense to ask great questions.

In the previous chapter, we learned that world-class teamwork often resulted when teams were challenged to solve problems collectively. Many organisations have problems to solve and questions to answer, but they don't engage their team by asking them specific questions.

How does this apply to you?

I have seen many board meeting agendas that contain a series of reports delivered by the directors. A significant proportion of the meeting is spent reporting on the status of various parts of the business. As the reports are delivered, people ask questions to seek clarity or challenge what they've heard. They might identify issues and assign somebody to address them. However, they don't often take the challenges that they face and collectively work on solutions. When you look at your meeting agendas, how many of them have, 'How could we?' or 'How can we?' questions? How many meetings are designed to engage the team in solving the issues together?

Interestingly, in many situations, we task individuals to provide solutions. We assume that a person, often with input from others, is best placed to solve the problems. We engage the 'experts' and those with the greatest experience in the hope that they will have an answer. Contrary to popular opinion, there is a strong body of evidence that suggests the best solutions come from crowds, not individuals. James Surowiecki demonstrates that in many situations, including the prediction of future trends, the crowd is consistently smarter than any one individual expert.[9] Interestingly, groups can also be less effective than individuals; Surowiecki points out that 'group think' tends not to be constructive. What, then, is the difference between a team that suffers from 'group think' and the wisdom of a crowd?

James Surowiecki explains that those teams who experience 'group think' often end up simply following those members who speak first or speak loudest. Social psychologist Solomon Asch found that many people in group settings will tend to conform with the majority, even when it means contradicting what they know to be the truth.[10] Of course, this negates the thinking power within the team. To avoid 'group think', and unlock the collective wisdom of the group, we need to aggregate the individual input from independent thinkers. We need to let people think for themselves, and then pool that input. The diversity in responses often provides the crowd with real power. James Surowiecki also understands that for a crowd to be truly wise it needs to have a very specific question.

Practise the challenge, not just the skills

Through my work as a sport psychology consultant and performance coach, I have become increasingly aware that both teams and individuals need to extend the scope of their practice beyond the perfection of skills. I was reminded of this again recently as I watched a very professional and talented team struggle to adapt to new demands. The solution that they were employing is one that would seem to make sense to many people. They were practising the skills that they felt they would need in competition.

This particular organisation is one of the best cricket teams in the world, and their challenge was to score more runs in the shortest competitive form of the game: Twenty20 cricket. Their answer, initially, was to practise the shots that they needed to play. In reality, though, they needed to practise the challenge that they were going to be facing. In Twenty20 cricket, bowlers tend to employ different tactics to restrict the number of runs that the opposition can score. The bowlers tend to bowl more 'yorkers', where they aim the ball at the batsmen's toes. It was this challenge that our batsmen struggled with. Although the batsmen could defend against these deliveries, they didn't score many runs and would often rely on the bowler executing their skill badly to find run-scoring opportunities.

How do they score more runs against this style of bowling? Rather than practising shots, perhaps a better solution would be to practise the challenge and find solutions to overcome it. As we

know, team performances are made up of individual performances. Therefore, we often need to practise both the skills and the
challenge as individuals, as well as collectively.

Debrief like the Red Arrows

In my experience, debriefs are relatively common. Good debriefs
are less common, great debriefs are pretty rare and world-class
debriefs are like hen's teeth. The Red Arrows are one team that
excel in this department, as we saw earlier. Whereas some teams
will review their performance on a weekly, monthly or quarterly
basis, the Red Arrows thoroughly debrief at the end of every day.
Like many world-class teams, they understand that debriefing
well allows them to learn from each performance and improve
upon it. This way, they become better today than they were yesterday, and better tomorrow than they are today.

How does this apply to you?

Many business leaders tell me that, unlike in sport and the military, they simply don't have the luxury of being able to practise
their performance or to debrief. They tell me that from start to
finish, they perform during every moment of every day so they
don't have time. I would argue that the gap between 'practice' and
'performance' is simply a matter of perception. In sport there are
days when we practise, and days when we compete. If we call
today 'a competition day' (because there is a trophy up for grabs),
does it mean that we cannot learn? If we call today 'a practice' does
it mean that we are not competing or aiming to produce our very
best performance? Is there really a difference? Could we decide to
simultaneously perform at our best *and* learn as much as possible,
regardless of whether we call this 'practice' or 'performance'?
I would suggest that businesses also have the opportunities to

practise and debrief like athletes and the military – they just need to look for them.

World-class leaders constantly reinforce the importance of reviewing and debriefing. A thorough, robust and brutally honest debrief seems to be absolutely central to their success. I would argue that we all have the opportunity to do this. Polar expedition leader Alan Chambers ensures that his team debrief in the tent, at -60 degrees Celsius, after a 28-hour day hauling their sleds across the Arctic. RAF pilots ensure they debrief each incident (including the near misses) after an intense combat mission. In both cases there must be a temptation to say, 'I haven't got the energy to debrief, I'm tired, let's just call it a day.' Crucially, the very best leaders don't choose to call it a day; they know that debriefing is just too important.

Captain Chesley Sullenberger, who landed his A320 in the Hudson River, explains that in civil aviation learning from mistakes is not a luxury – it is a duty: 'Everything we know has been learned because someone died, or many died. These lessons have come at the greatest cost. We cannot have the moral failure of forgetting these lessons.'

He also acknowledges that this constant debrief-and-learning process helped him avoid a fatal catastrophe when his engines lost thrust seconds after take-off: 'Over many decades, thousands of people in aviation have worked very hard to create a robust resilient safety system on which to operate, and that formed the firm foundation on which we could innovate and improvise to solve this crisis.'[11]

A world-class debrief

What differentiates a good debrief from a great debrief, and a great debrief from a world-class debrief?

I have noticed that the very best debrief-and-review sessions have four characteristics: frequency, depth, brutal honesty and accountability. Depth comes when we delve deeper, asking follow-up questions that give us ever-greater clarity. Many teams will ask, 'What did we do well, and what could we do better?' That's a good start. I've been working with a world-class cricket team recently who used to ask those questions, but that's where it ended. Recently, we have been working to evolve the debrief and increase the depth of the questions. The team's job is simply to score as many runs as possible, and bowl the opposition out for as few runs as possible. Therefore, our questions are focused on assessing our performance in these two areas:

1   Did we score as many runs as possible?

2   Did we bowl the opposition out for as few runs as possible?

3   How many more runs could we have scored?

4   How many fewer runs could we have conceded?

5   Where did we have opportunities to score runs that we didn't take?

6   Where did we have opportunities to restrict runs or take wickets sooner?

7   How good was our game plan?

8   How well did we execute it?

9   How well did we perform today, on a scale of 0–10?

10   What did we do well, which we're going to keep doing (i.e. the reason we didn't score zero)?

11   What do we need to improve (i.e. the gap between our performance and a 10)?

12 What do *we* (collectively) need to do differently? What are *we* going to change next time?

13 What are *you* (individually) going to change?

14 How will we know when we get there?

15 What will we see and hear differently next time?

16 What are *we* going to commit to doing?

17 What are *you* going to commit to doing?

In addition to greater depth, the follow-up questions also begin to ask what we are going to do differently and what individuals will do differently. By understanding what we will see and hear differently next time, we also have a tangible way of holding each other accountable for making the changes we need. This process alone becomes a powerful way of instigating improvements in performance. That power is increased when the team members are willing to be completely, and sometimes brutally, honest with each other. Brutal honesty is one of the six characteristics of world-class teams that we identified in the opening chapter. The debrief is one of the forums in which we can develop the level of honesty. Interestingly, the Red Arrows encourage this in a very simple way. As I mentioned earlier, each debrief begins with the leader outlining what they think they could have done better. They then invite other members of the team to share their views on the leader's performance. This simple act then gives the rest of the team licence to identify where they could also improve. The All Blacks have a saying: 'Stab me in the front.' It is a request. They are asking each other for constructive, critical feedback because they know it will improve their performance.[12]

I often see a progression in the level of brutal honesty within teams. It begins when individuals are willing to put their hand up and say, 'I think I could have done X better.' As the level of honesty increases, team members are also able to say, 'I think you could have done X better.' It's often easier and more comfortable for people to recognise their own shortcomings than to point out those of other people. With this level of honesty, we can build accountability. Once we have identified what each person needs to do differently, we can then hold each other to account for delivering this. When teams begin to do this, I often hear them saying, 'Come on, you told us that you needed to do X better and that you were going to spend time practising it. Let's see it. We're all doing what we agreed to do. If you want to be part of this team, you need to do the same.'

Oh, and don't forget . . .

Sir Clive Woodward explained his very simple formula for turning the England Rugby Team from consistent under-achievers into world champions. From the very beginning Clive emphasised the need for fun – yes, fun. He underlined that the environment needed to be one that the players wanted to be a part of and sought to be involved in. Therefore, the players needed to enjoy being in that environment.[13] Of course, Clive Woodward is not alone. English Premier League manager Tony Pulis is reported to have prioritised 'raising spirits' when he took over an ailing Crystal Palace team.[14] Victorious skipper Brendan Hall prioritised crew morale and the need to make the boat 'a great place to be'.[15] To help make it happen, he appointed a crew member to be the 'morale officer' aboard *Spirit of Australia*.

There are many different ways in which we can increase the fun factor without compromising the quality of the work. I've spoken to many leaders who refer to the need for 'serious fun'. It is a term that emphasises the need for seriousness as well as enjoyment and also their desire to make it really good fun –

serious fun, in fact. Clive Woodward introduced music into training sessions, for example. He understood that often the work rate, tempo, intensity and endurance increased just by adding music. Many leaders also understand that people's enjoyment tends to peak when there is a balance between the challenge that they're presented with and their skills.[16] To be more precise, humans perform at their best, and enjoy what they do, when there is a balance between their perception of the challenge and their perception of their own skills. When we begin to understand our team in more depth, we begin to see how they respond to challenges. We can also see where their comfort zone ends and their discomfort zone begins. Talking to them about their experiences also helps us to understand their level of enjoyment. All this information helps us to create an environment that is fun!

Summary

Improving performance requires effort, energy and focus. It demands more of us, so people often need a strong reason to break the status quo and improve. When teams are in crisis, this reason is often obvious. The greater challenge often comes when the going is good. Perhaps the best reason to improve is because it is what we do every day. Great teams are often constantly looking for ways to refine their processes. They realise that increased results depend on better processes. Leaders focus on improving briefings, debriefs, planning, preparation and practice, which delivers greater performances. They raise the bar by upping both the challenge and the support in tandem. In doing so, they can also encourage the team to search for that next inch and to ensure that they don't compromise the tiny details. Great questions, and a really honest debrief, help to engage the team in solving the problems and meeting the challenges.

- Identify your reason. Your team needs a strong reason to improve, because improving will require more effort. Improvement should be a constant. By improving performance, we also tend to make life easier and give the team members greater satisfaction.

- It is essential to be focused, confident and motivated, but to do well we need to have the knowledge, skills, resources and the desire to do it. If we understand our job, we also stand a very good chance of performing well. Identify the key processes you need to focus on to do that job.

- Evaluate your performance regularly, after every match or every business day. Ask yourself: how good was my game plan? How well did I execute it? Become more interested in the processes, and focus on them completely to improve.

- Use briefings to provide clarity.

- Increase your support for members of your team at the same time as you increase the challenge. Introduce challenges steadily rather than suddenly. Think about improving performance one inch at a time and be sure to get the basics right.

- Post a specific and well-defined question to engage the team, and give them ownership over the problem. Ask great questions if you are looking for great answers, because these will guide the team's thinking.

- Team performances are made up of individual performances, so practise both the skills and the challenge as individuals as well as collectively.

- Debrief regularly and thoroughly to develop the level of honesty and to build accountability. Include the four characteristics: frequency, depth, brutal honesty and accountability.

- We perform at our best and enjoy what we do when there is a balance between our perception of the challenge and the perception of our skills.

WORKSHOP: Improving team performance

Take a moment to reflect on what you see in your team at the moment. Score your team using the simple 0–10 scale. As before, a score of 10 means 'perfect, flawless, cannot be improved'. A score of zero means that there is nothing good about it.

How would you rate:

1   Your compelling reason to improve all the time?
2   The improvement in individual performances?
3   Your ability to raise standards, not just targets?
4   Your ability to create clarity by focusing on processes and the use of effective briefings.
5   The quality of your practices and debriefs?

CHAPTER 6

World-class Leadership

Leadership has several different levels. Commonly, when we think of leadership we focus on the leader. We often see the leader as the one individual who is in overall charge of the team. Interestingly, high-performing teams often have many layers of leadership – even those with just a handful of members. Some teams are actually referred to as 'a team of leaders'. These teams are often capable of delivering exceptional performances in adverse and volatile conditions, because their depth of leadership allows them to be incredibly resilient and responsive.

A team of leaders

In some cases, there is a very strong functional need to have a team of leaders. Special Forces units often operate in the knowledge that they could lose their primary leader. If losing the team leader rendered them rudderless, the unit would be incredibly vulnerable. US Navy SEAL team leader, Gary Rossi, explained how their preparation was designed to ensure the entire team could become leaders.

> Before we embarked on any mission, the team would always be taken into secure confinement. If we had orders

to go on a Monday, we'd go into confinement on, say, the Friday night and we start preparing – no calls, no contact with the outside world. We have a warning order which gives us some idea of what we need to get together. Then we go into a detailed Patrol Leader's Order. It's like a strategic plan. It goes into the terrain, it goes into the geography, insertion, extraction, what weapons do we need, what's the countryside, who are the friendlies, who are the enemies, are we parachuting in, are we going to extract via submarine? It goes into so many levels of excruciating detail so nothing is left to chance. Each of us has a function, each of us has a role and a responsibility. We know the chain of command. I knew that if I was third most senior, if we lost the top two guys, I was in command and I was ready to go. I had to know the plan as well as the leader. And if we don't get these tiny details absolutely right, the smallest thing can cause an absolute catastrophe.[1]

In his book, *Elite!*, Floyd Woodrow describes an SAS mission behind enemy lines in Iraq. The leader of Delta Eight Unit was shot and wounded during the mission and needed to be airlifted to a field hospital. Immediately, the second-in-command stepped up and took the reins.[2] Of course, this doesn't happen by chance. It happens because the entire team are developed as leaders. Therefore, leading a team is second nature to them. They also practise and prepare for these eventualities, because there is a high likelihood that they'll need to change the leadership at very short notice. The new leader is prepared to take over, and the team is prepared for a new leader.

It is not just Special Forces units that operate as a team of leaders, however. The same is true in racing yacht crews. As the skipper of a Clipper Round the World Yacht Race crew, Brendan Hall invested a great deal of time ensuring that his crew would be capable of sailing the boat to a safe port if he was incapacitated.[3] He deliberately sought to step back and gradually give the crew greater responsibility for decision-making and execution. He schooled his watch leaders to be able to sail the boat without being dependent on his input. In fact, he describes working towards a position where he would become more of a consultant to the crew. Incredibly, during the race, Brendan needed to call upon this when he was asked to transfer to an opposing boat whose skipper was badly injured. It meant that his crew were able to sail safely through hurricane conditions in the treacherous North Pacific without him.

America's Cup helmsman Andy Beadsworth also described how world-class yacht crews will often adopt different leaders during the race, as situations change.

> When we work well, we follow a fairly simple process. Job one is to recognise the situation. It could be someone in the middle of the boat who has the best viewpoint. Who has the information? Sometimes it is best for them to take the lead. Sometimes we need the information to come back to the skipper or leader to make the decisions. If I am skipper, I may hand over leadership to the person at the sharp end and ask what he needs – 'You take over, what do you need?' At any point, anyone on the boat can shout 'Hold, hold, hold, I've seen X.'

The importance of individuals' leadership roles

This fluid system of leadership obviously requires a basis of trust and respect throughout the team. It also depends upon having a leader who is willing to hand over control when there is someone better placed to lead. As James Surowiecki reports, although the US Army is thought of as an organisation that's led from the top down, the reality is very different.[4] They know that local knowledge is powerful, so commanders on the ground are given considerable latitude to make decisions based on what they see in front of them, and then act. This doesn't mean that the units become uncoordinated and disconnected. Their communication systems actually allow the organisation as a whole to function a bit like a body. Our bodies have sensory organs, which detect what is happening in our environment. We have a nervous system that relays messages back to the central command system (our thinking brain), and then sends messages back to the working muscles that guide our movement. We also have unconscious processes and reflexes that shortcut this and allow our bodies to respond immediately to our environment without the need for our brains to make decisions. Our balance, temperature regulation and many other functions are governed without the need for commands from our thinking brain. Importantly, even when our reflexes kick in, the sensory organs inform our brain so that we know what's happening at our extremities.

When I look at highly effective organisations at work, I see similar patterns. Sir Clive Woodward explained that England rugby had eight leaders on the field in a team of 15 players.[5] Each had a very specific leadership role. First, there was the captain, who was responsible for ensuring that all the players are 'as one' with the philosophy. The fly-half, scrum-half and number 8 (in that order), were responsible for ensuring that the team played to the game plan, and adapted to changes as they were presented. These players were the directional leaders on the field. They assessed the relative strengths and weaknesses of each team and engineered the game to maximise their own strengths and expose the opposition's weaknesses. One of the front row forwards was responsible for the performance of the scrum, including the calls. One of the lock forwards was responsible for the performance in the line-out, including the calls. The inside centre was responsible for defensive positions of the backs. The open-side flanker was responsible for defensive positions of the forwards. As Clive Woodward says, 99 per cent of this work happened in training, team meetings, phone calls with other players and staff, and time spent studying the opposition. This foundation allowed it to translate onto the field on match day.

When we view leadership in this way, we often get a much broader perspective. It is distinctly different from the narrow 'one person as leader' approach.

The leadership team

Many teams, even relatively small teams, will have a distinct leadership team. This team often comprises two or three of the more senior members. The leadership team often serve a number of valuable functions. They act as an extended brain for the primary leader, providing a sounding board for thoughts and ideas. Sometimes this provides the leader with a sanity check. On other occasions, it is a way of getting specialist input from others who have different strengths and expertise. It is also a good way for a leader to extend their sensory awareness through the eyes and ears of others. This helps them to keep their fingers on the pulse of the team, to gauge the mood and to understand how team members are thinking and feeling.

Brendan Hall describes the way he selected his leadership team on *Spirit of Australia*.[6] Importantly, he knew that he needed to select the best leaders, not the best sailors. He understood that people-management, and managing the expectations of the crew, were critically important to their success. Brendan also explains that he sought people who would complement his own strengths and weaknesses. After assessing his own leadership style, Brendan knew that it was based on good negotiating skills. Naturally, he would negotiate and consult with his crew.

Therefore, when selecting watch leaders to make up his leadership team, Brendan chose those who had a more directive and supportive style. In his view, a leader might struggle to be completely rounded. However, by finding others who complement our style, we can develop a well-rounded leadership team.

The captain of a sports team asked me how he could engage those members of the team who had very different personalities from his own. The captain was a true 'sergeant major', as I described on page 64. He was very focused, very competitive and decisive. Some members of the team were 'hippies', who valued relationships and harmony. Typically, this particular captain doesn't mind conflict. The hippies, on the other hand, tend to avoid conflict. Sometimes they perceive that sergeant majors are too hasty, unilateral and abrupt. Conversely, the sergeant majors often get frustrated if the hippies seem indecisive, non-urgent, lethargic or slow to act.

The solution, for the captain, was to tap into the strengths of other senior players. One of the players, in particular, had a personality that was much closer to the hippies. He understood the need to think about the human impact of any decision, and how it is delivered. In addition to the tactical impact of a decision, this player understood how it was likely to make people feel. By widening the leadership team, and including other players who could complement him, the captain found that they were better able to engage the whole team.

Leadership teams are often better placed to make great decisions than any one individual. Multiple perspectives can help. It is often beneficial to blend people who might be higher risk-takers with those who are more conservative. Balancing decisiveness with critical questioning and analytical thinking can give us enormous value. It is rare for one person to provide all the qualities necessary. However, a well-balanced leadership team is far more likely to contain these.

Influential leaders

Why should a team follow the leader? Is it simply because they wear the captain's armband, have more stripes on their epaulettes or have a plate with the letters 'CEO' on the door? If we think about it rationally, those are not particularly good reasons for us to follow leaders. I recently wrote a book called *How to Herd Cats*, which identifies how leaders can galvanise a group of independent thinkers to become a cohesive team. To herd cats, we need to remember that independent thinkers will make their own decisions, according to their self-interest. It is a principle that is illustrated perfectly in animal teams.

Interestingly, animal teams seem to have a very simple and highly effective method of choosing their leaders. Leaders in the animal kingdom are not self-selected, or chosen by an exclusive group. Very simply, the leader is the one that the other animals choose to follow. If a group of animals are searching for food, they will tend to follow the individual who is most likely to know where the food is – the one with the knowledge and experience. For example, if there is one individual who knows how to navigate to a particularly good spot, the others will follow them. Bees are remarkably efficient at finding food, even over relatively large distances, so how does a colony of bees ensure that they collectively make the most of the available food sources? Is it a case of every bee for himself? Do they randomly fly until they find food? If one bee finds a good source of food, are they the only one to benefit? Or is there a way of helping the whole colony to find it? How does the colony know which sources of food are the best?

The bees' answer is to send out foragers or scouts. These bees then communicate the quality of the food source they have found by way of a 'waggle dance'. The intensity of the dance relates directly to the quality of the food source (such as the nectar available in a patch of flowers). Therefore, the other foragers will follow on a second visit those bees that displayed the strongest dances. Some bees will therefore have more followers than others. The lead bees then set off to their chosen areas with their band of followers. After several more scouting missions and displays of waggle dancing, the bees will have narrowed down to the best source of food. By default, they will all have chosen to follow one of the bees to their source of food. Importantly, the waggle dance is not a popularity contest for the bees. There is no benefit to each bee in becoming the leader. The only benefit comes if they all find the strongest food source. Therefore, there is no interest in bees performing a great waggle dance in order to recruit followers. In animal teams, leadership tends to be allocated on a very functional basis. Human beings confuse this very elegant process, by introducing their ego. Often people want to become the leader because it carries more status, importance and even reward.

This wisdom is not confined to the animal kingdom, although arguably it's more common to find it in animals than humans. RAF fighter pilot Mandy Hickson explained that operational missions are not necessarily led by the officer with the highest rank.[7] Instead, they are led by the person with the greatest knowledge or level of expertise for that particular mission. Because they are better placed to do so, it is not unusual to find lower-ranking officers leading those of a higher rank.

How do you spot the leader?

Sometimes the most profound insights come when you least expect them. During a conversation with animal-teams expert Dr Dan Franks, I asked how you identify the leader in a flock of pigeons. 'Is the leader the pigeon at the front?', I asked. Dan told me that it could be the bird at the front, but it doesn't have to be. Pigeons, like most birds, don't have eyes that point forwards.

Instead they have eyes on the sides of their heads, which provide more of a 360-degree perspective. Therefore, the leader doesn't need to be at the front to be seen, they can be anywhere within the flock, and they could fly in the middle. How, then, can you tell which bird is leading? The truth is very simple, and it provided a 'light bulb moment' for me:

> The leader is the one to whom the most attention is directed.

> When the lead pigeon banks to the left, the flock follows.

This understanding can help us to identify the real leaders in the organisation. If I'm looking for the leaders, I don't tend to focus on their job titles. Instead, I look for the amount of influence they have on those around them. Former England football team manager Sven-Göran Eriksson used the term 'cultural architects' to describe those who influenced the organisation. These are the people who have the ability to shape the culture and are often the real leaders. If we think about this in more depth, it gives a very clear view of leadership. If we understand leadership in the same way that animals do, we come to two fundamental truths:

1   Leaders are elected by those who choose to follow them.

2   Leaders are those who influence the people around them.

The characteristics of great leaders

As you might imagine, I've been reading plenty of books and articles on great leadership. Unsurprisingly, I've found hundreds of different accounts from a host of leadership gurus across the ages. In around 500BC, Chinese military general Sun Tzu observed in his book *The Art of War* that there were five great virtues of leadership:

> Leadership is a matter of intelligence, trustworthiness, humaneness, courage, and discipline. Reliance on intelligence alone results in rebelliousness. Exercise of humaneness alone results in weakness. Fixation on trust results in folly. Dependence on the strength of courage results in violence. Excessive discipline and sternness in command result in cruelty. When one has all five virtues together, each appropriate to its function, then one can be a leader.[8]

More recently, author and speaker Brendon Burchard describes what great leaders actually do through his 'six Es'.[9] Having seen many lists of leadership characteristics, I have to admit that these are as good as any I have seen. To be honest, I wish I'd come up with them first. His six Es are:

Envision Great leaders have the vision. They know what tomorrow should look like and how it will be better. They know the mission, the cause, the compelling purpose and why it's important. And, they share this with others.

Enlist Great leaders enlist other people to help make the vision a reality. In doing so, they go beyond attracting followers. Instead, they engage co-creators and collaborators, who happily invest themselves in helping to make the vision a reality.

Embody Great leaders are the living, breathing embodiment of their vision and message. They ensure that everything they do reinforces, supports and reflects their message.

As Brendon Burchard says, 'You won't believe the message, if you don't believe the messenger.'

Empower Great leaders enable others to deliver by empowering them. This goes beyond giving them permission. It also means providing them with the skills, the knowledge, the tools, the resources and the confidence to deliver.

Evaluate Great leaders evaluate the position, to assess whether the team is on track and whether they're actually turning the vision into reality. In doing so, they'll take input from others, and give feedback to others.

Encourage Great leaders, as Brendon Burchard describes them, are 'the champions, the cheerleaders and the motivators'. Of course, that's easy enough to do at the beginning and when things are going well. It's much harder to do consistently if you're on a long-haul journey, and it can be especially challenging during those dark times when things get really tough.

A Google search will provide you with hundreds, if not thousands, of other examples. Each has a slightly different perspective on leadership. My own interpretation of great leadership is based on my personal observations and conversations with the world-class leaders that I've met. As I tried to conceptualise what I saw them doing, a pattern began to emerge.

World-class leaders answer the *why?*, *what?*, *how?*, *when?* and *who?*

Why? As author Simon Sinek explains, leaders inspire because they emphasise 'the why?'.[10] Sinek uses examples such as Dr Martin Luther King and Steve Jobs. These are leaders who engage people because they focus on *why?*. Dr Martin Luther King shared his *why?* when he told a nation, 'I have a dream.' As Sri Lankan cricket coach Paul Farbrace explained, their World Cup campaign was fuelled by a desire to win for their two retiring players. Simon Sinek emphasises that 'people don't buy what you do, they buy why you do it'. Great leaders are focused on the purpose and communicate this to their teams. When leaders share their *why?*, it allows people to align their personal purpose to that of the team. Importantly, it enables people to identify with the cause and to commit to it.

What? The world-class leaders that I've seen also understand what they do with clarity and simplicity. Therefore, they are able to pass this understanding on to their teams. Fred Smith at FedEx created clarity for the whole organisation when he said their job was simply to deliver a package overnight.[11] Equally, the SAS teams that liberated the Iranian Embassy had a very clear job: to rescue the hostages in the building.[12] The *Spirit of Australia* crew were simply asking, 'Does it make the boat go quicker?'[13] In short, the leader knows the 'two lengths of the pool' and helps the team to understand it too.

As individuals, when we have a simple, clear task, we have a good chance of doing that job well. The same is true when we operate in a team. As well as helping to clarify the job of the team, great leaders ensure that each individual knows exactly what they are supposed to do and how it contributes to the team as a whole.

Many leaders confuse the issue by pushing their team to deliver a result or an outcome-related target. Sports coaches often tell their team to go out and win. Sales managers tell their team to hit the sales target. When we do this, we often give our teams a task that is beyond their control. In many cases, the net result is that our people feel under pressure and therefore deliver a below-par performance.

It doesn't mean that we simply tell the team to do their best and then sit with our fingers crossed. UK Sport performance director, Simon Timson, outlined how GB Olympic programmes analyse what they need to do to win, and then create a plan to deliver the processes required. Their research demonstrated that to win the Men's 1,500m in an Olympic final, athletes would need to complete the last lap in under 52 seconds. There are potentially hundreds of things that contribute to success in the 1,500m, but UK Sport knew that this element was crucial. Therefore, enabling athletes to complete a sub-52-second last 400m became a key focus for the training programme.

Who? Once we know the job of the team in the simplest possible terms, we can also see how each individual is best able to contribute to it. Great leaders know their people; they understand who has the skills, the aptitude, the mentality, the personality and the interest in each task. I suspect that many leaders would focus primarily on the skills and possibly the aptitude first. The great leaders that I have observed definitely look to play people to their strengths and find ways to enable them to perform at their best. Although I would agree that assigning tasks based on skills and aptitude is important, I would also advocate looking further. Who is most interested, curious or passionate about this job? Who wants to do it? Who cares about it?

When? The very best leaders that I have seen also understand the strategic needs of the team and the project. They have that 'helicopter view' which allows them to know when the various pieces of the jigsaw need to fall into place. There is a temptation to become impatient and task people to do everything as quickly as possible. I have seen many bosses who always want it done 'Now!' or even 'Yesterday!' Invariably, this leads the team to become frantic and hasty. They feel like they're racing out of control. It's like that sensation you get when you're driving along at high speed. Everything looks like a blur. You don't have time to respond to things well, because they seem to hit you all of a sudden. As soon as one crisis has been averted, the next one is upon you. Great leaders stop and ask, 'When do we actually need to deliver this?' Sometimes that means gathering information from outside the team. Once they have this information, and understand the strategic needs, they can ask much more empowering questions of the team.

The Red Arrows' formula for empowerment is very simple. As Jas Hawker described it: 'We give them the what and the when by, they decide upon how.' In order to adopt this simple and highly effective approach, you have to know both what to ask the team for, and when by. Simply barking 'Now!' or 'Yesterday!' is not a great solution.

How? Once we know *why?* and *what?*, we can set about creating a plan to provide the *how?*. Interestingly, it is on this point that many of the leadership gurus differ. Should the leader provide the plan? Should they set the strategy? Or, should they engage the team to find the *how?* Although some would propose that the leader should provide their team with the plan, others disagree. In his book, *Elite!*, Floyd Woodrow explains (in the box below) that although SAS team leaders facilitate the process, it is the units that collectively create the plan.

Behind enemy lines – two approaches

Delta Eight and Delta Nine are two units that were deployed behind enemy lines in Iraq. These two teams were in the same place, at the same time, with the same brief and the same resources available to them. Logic would suggest that the two teams would achieve similar levels of success. Crucially, there was one fundamental difference; the way the two units were led.

▶

Martin, the leader of Delta Eight, took time to understand his team, their personalities and their skills. He knew that there was a wealth of skills, experience and knowledge that would be valuable in creating their mission plan. Martin engaged his team by giving them the brief, setting them the challenge and collectively producing a strategy. He also knew that there were some members of the team who tended to be quieter and more reserved. These people didn't tend to volunteer their views in group discussions, but they did have valuable input. Therefore, Martin deliberately asked their opinions and sought their input. During the course of the planning exercise, there was some healthy disagreement. Importantly, everyone knew that their views had been taken into account, so when the time came to submit the plan, everyone committed to it.

Over in Delta Nine the leader, Jim, brought his team together and presented them with the brief. As with Delta Eight, there was a great deal of discussion. Delta Nine also had some quieter members with experience and knowledge, but their voices seemed to be drowned out by the more vocal members of the team. There seemed to be a small group of supporters forming around Jim, who endorsed his plan. By default, the plan was accepted. The dominance of a few members nullified the quiet dissenters.

During their missions, both Delta Eight and Delta Nine encountered significant adversity. Delta Eight successfully completed the first part of their mission before encountering an enemy battalion. During the course of the gun battle their leader, Martin, was shot and wounded. Immediately, Plan B kicked in and his number two stepped up. They called in support and Martin was evacuated to a field hospital. Whenever

▶

there was a change, the team came together, co-created a new plan and then committed to it. Their plan was not the leader's plan; it was the team's plan.

Delta Nine's problems began when they landed behind enemy lines. They landed in an exposed location and were forced to march with heavy kit in driving rain and freezing temperatures so that they could find safety. This meant that they began the mission with a wet, cold, hungry and vulnerable team. The team began to fire-fight problems. Instead of progressing through their mission, they were dealing with issues. When morale starts to drop, little problems become big problems. Issues compound. There were mutterings of discontent; the leader's plan was not working!

There tends to be a domino effect. Negative thoughts form inside people's minds. These thoughts are then voiced and become mutterings. Soon, cliques started to form and team members began to dissent and challenge the leadership. As a result the leader, Jim, started to become defensive and snapped at the team. Instead of being a unified team, Delta Nine became fragmented and began to blame the leader for their situation and performance. The story ends as Delta Eight, minus the wounded Martin, are tasked to rescue Delta Nine, who have become locked down by the enemy.[14]

Leaders who empower

Empowerment is a commonly used term within leadership and teamwork these days. Many leaders know the importance of empowering their people and aspire to do it. But, when it comes to the crunch, they don't seem able to turn the intentions into reality. Often the challenge arises when the leader needs to relinquish some control. If the leader perceives that they are the most skilled or knowledgeable person in the team, they may conclude that giving control to others equates to a drop in standards. I have spoken to many leaders who say, 'By the time I've taught someone else to do it to the right standard, I could have done it myself ten times.' The catch-22, of course, is that if you choose to do it yourself, you will end up doing it more than ten times. If we empower others, there is a risk that the standards may drop initially. Many leaders are conscious that they cannot afford that. In some cases, leaders would genuinely love to empower their people but can't find the time or the opportunity to do it.

World-class leaders seem to understand that empowering others requires planning. The key question seems to be 'When is the best time?' When time is pre-planned, it is less likely to be disruptive to the leader. Therefore, both the leader and the team members can devote the time needed to do the job properly. There may also be opportunities to enable people to pick up the reins during steady periods, when there is less demand. Normally, this gives us slightly more margin for error and allows people to make mistakes as they learn.

Often really effective coaching processes are pretty simple. It starts with instruction: I do it; you watch and ask questions. The process then moves on to supervision: you do it; I watch and give feedback. Then we take another step back: you do it; I check and give feedback, if necessary. Gradually, leaders feel less need to check and therefore begin to trust. Of course, the door is always open if the team member needs some advice or a second opinion.

In some cases, leaders spend time talking through decisions, so that both they and the team member understand the thought process in the same way. In yacht crews, often the skipper will start by making decisions with crew members. This dialogue allows the crew members to know how decisions are made and what factors the skipper is considering. Over a short period of time, the crew members understand the decision-making process and can second-guess what the skipper would do. The same principle can be used when executing processes. Brendan Hall describes how he would brief the crew, listen to them performing a manoeuvre, wait until they'd completed it, and then come up onto the deck and congratulate them on a job well done.[15]

Of course, the leader develops confidence in the team when they see the team performing. Naturally, when the leader has confidence in their people, the people begin to develop confidence in themselves.

San Antonio Spurs basketball coach, Gregg Popovich, revealed that during a time-out he will often refrain from pulling out the white board and the marker pens. His approach is very different from most coaches. Rather than providing the players with answers, he'll often say nothing and allow them to take control. He has been with the core group of veterans long enough to trust that they know their game plan and that they will figure out what will work best on the court. He puts the responsibility for decision-making and execution in the hands of his players. Of course, ultimately, it is the players who will deliver.[16] Although this might seem like an obvious route to take, many coaches feel compelled to intervene. After all, it's their job on the line. As the leader, they are responsible for delivering results. They will be blamed if the team loses. Despite the weight of expectation, Gregg Popovich understands the need to empower the team and allow them to deliver the solutions.

Leadership is about service, not power

Field Marshall Bill Slim was a British military commander who led the so-called 'forgotten army' in Burma during World War II. In talking to his officers about leadership, he said: 'Officers are there to lead. I tell you, therefore, as officers, that you will neither eat, nor drink, nor sleep, nor smoke, nor even sit down until you have personally seen that your men have done those things. If you will do this for them, they will follow you to the end of the world.'

Field Marshall Slim recognised that a leader's role is to look after and care for his or her people. He doesn't see people as a tool for getting the job done. He sees them as valuable partners. The leader's role is to help and enable them to perform at their best and therefore to advance the collective cause. Jack Welch, CEO of global giant General Electric, said, 'Before you are a leader, success is all about growing yourself. When you become a leader, success is all about growing others.' He also identifies a shift in emphasis for those taking positions of leadership: 'It's not about you anymore, it is about them.'[17]

The term 'servant leadership' was coined in the 1970s by Robert Greenleaf, but the concept dates back thousands of years. Chinese philosopher Lao Tzu is quoted as saying:

> The highest type of ruler is one of whose existence the people are barely aware. Next comes one whom they love and praise. Next comes one whom they fear. Next comes one whom they despise and defy ... The Sage is self-effacing and scanty of words. When his task is accomplished and things have been completed, all the people say, 'We ourselves have achieved it!'[18]

In his book, *Leadership is an Art*, Max DePree says, 'The first responsibility of a leader is to define reality. The last is to say thank you. In between, the leader is a servant.'[19]

Interestingly the word *samurai*, which is associated with Japanese warriors, actually means 'to serve'.[20] In my work with world-class teams and leaders, I have often heard the leader asking their team members, 'What can I do to help you?' This question is born out of a genuine and intrinsic belief that their role is to do whatever they can to help their people perform. In doing so, they see themselves as an assistant in that process. It is very different from the view that leaders have 'power'. I would certainly agree that great leaders have enormous influence. Arguably, with influence comes power. However, it seems that great leaders do not seek leadership in order to wield power or advance themselves. It seems that they do so in order to better serve others and the collective cause.

'Everybody can be great, because everybody can serve'
Dr Martin Luther King

See the bigger picture

Fighter pilot Mandy Hickson described the leader as a Sherpa (Himalayan mountain guide).[21] The Sherpa's job is to lead the team to the peak of the mountain and get everyone back safely. To do that, they need to help everyone in the team achieve their potential. When everyone else is performing and delivering, it gives the leader the headspace to see the bigger picture. If a leader is micromanaging, they are often so embroiled in the minutiae that they fail to see dangers on the horizon. In a crisis, the leader needs 'situational awareness'. This is the ability to take a step back and see developments unfolding. Leaders often lose this ability because they become overloaded. Developing situational awareness often comes when we give ourselves the ability to look up.

The personal characteristics of world-class leaders

As with many areas of leadership there are hundreds, if not thousands, of different interpretations of the personal characteristics that great leaders display. Through my work and studies I have seen a handful of personal characteristics consistently. Of course, mine is not an exclusive list. I see these principles displayed in some of the world's greatest leaders, throughout history, and I firmly believe that they provide a solid foundation for world-class leadership.

Authenticity Put simply, great leaders know themselves and are happy to be themselves. They know who they are, and who they are not. Often, there is a genuine awareness that they're not perfect. Importantly, they are not trying to be perfect either. When people find it difficult to be themselves, I often hear them saying, 'I was trying to be ... ' It shows that they are attempting to be something other than what they are. Of course, we don't need to try to be ourselves, because it comes naturally. Great leaders are comfortable in their own skin. They don't tend to feel a pressure to do anything more, or be anything more, in order to be successful.

Values driven Often, there is a tension between our values and the need to deliver results. In sport, there is a temptation to cheat in an attempt to gain an advantage. In life we might choose to tell a little white lie in order to avoid embarrassing ourselves. Do we choose to sacrifice our margins to deliver a better service or protect profitability? Great leaders seem to consistently make choices that are driven by values, rather than an alternative agenda. It is because of this that great leaders display courage, wisdom, honesty and integrity. By doing so, they develop relationships that are based on trust and respect.

Caring Great leaders also show that they have a deep and genuine care for the people that they lead. This does not mean that they're 'soft', or that they tolerate sloppy standards or below-par performance. However, it does mean that they consider what's in the best interests of their people. This allows them to be selfless rather than selfish. It also means that they listen. I was recently asked how we can best develop listening skills. My answer, very simply, was to be genuinely interested and to care.

Respect choice How do great leaders manage to display genuine care for people without allowing standards to drop? In many cases, they manage to achieve both through an acute understanding of where each person's responsibility lies. They understand that we will never change other people. Human beings will always choose to change themselves, or not. Great leaders understand that each person has the choice to change and is therefore given responsibility for their own performance. It also means that leaders give each person the right to either succeed or fail. Although the team member is ultimately responsible for their performance, the leader provides the support.

Humility and humbleness Being humble, and displaying humility, does not mean that people are devoid of character or charisma. Often people see inspirational leaders as those who have a 'big personality' – those people who seem to be in their element on a stage, in front of a crowd. It is quite possible for leaders to have these qualities and to still remain humble. Humility sits at the opposite end of a spectrum to arrogance. Leaders who are humble recognise that their contribution is a part of the whole and is not more important than everyone else's. Therefore they value their own contributions alongside those of other people, not in a hierarchy.

When leaders do feel the need to prove themselves, they might try to do so through the performance of their team. In essence, the leader needs the team to deliver results in order to satisfy his or her own ego and self-worth. There is often a knock-on effect when leaders need the team to deliver results: they begin to feel pressure. The leader's thoughts and emotions manifest into negative behaviours when they start barking at their people to deliver results. Conversely, when leaders display a blend of humility, humbleness, care, values and authenticity, you see people that are not egotistical or self-centred. They don't feel the need to prove anything to anyone else.

Summary

Leadership is founded on influence, not orders or instructions. Great leadership is often not a solo exercise. The best teams are often described as a team of leaders. Often the greatest leadership comes from a leadership team, rather than a single individual. Some of the best teams adopt a fluid system, in which leadership switches, and the team follows the person who is best placed to lead at that moment. In order to adopt these approaches, leaders must empower their people. They must actively develop confidence in their people and be happy to share control. When I see great leaders at work, I do not see those who are power hungry and egotistical. Instead, I see people who serve with care, compassion and humility.

- Leadership requires a basis of trust and respect throughout the team. A good leader will be willing to hand over control when there is someone better placed to lead.

- We can learn from leadership in the animal kingdom, which tends to be allocated on a functional basis. To choose a suitable leader, don't focus on their job title, but look for the amount of influence they have on those around them. Remember that leaders are elected by those who choose to follow them, and they, in turn, influence the people around them.

- Before asking more empowering questions of the team, look at the basics of *why?*, *what?* and *when?*. Leaders inspire because they emphasise *why* and they understand *what* they do with clarity and simplicity. They play people to their strengths and find ways to enable them to perform at their best. They ask, *when* something needs to be achieved.

- A good leader should empower others. Use steady periods rather than times when the pressure is on to allow people to take over leadership roles and to learn through their mistakes. A leader who has confidence in the team will help team members to develop confidence in themselves.

- Look for the qualities that great leaders possess: they don't feel the need to prove anything to anyone else; they do not seek leadership to wield power or advance themselves but to serve others and the collective cause; they consistently make choices that are driven by values rather than an alternative agenda; they consider what's in the best interests of their teams and are genuinely interested in the individuals; they understand that each person has the choice to change and they give them responsibility for their own performance.

WORKSHOP: World-class leadership

Reflect on what you see in your leadership at the moment. Take a moment and score your leadership using the simple 0–10 scale. As before, a score of 10 means 'perfect, flawless, cannot be improved'. A score of zero means that there is nothing good about it.

How would you rate:

▶

1   The depth of leadership?
2   The ability to switch leaders and adopt fluid leadership?
3   The balance of your leadership team?
4   Your leader's strength of influence?
5   The use of Brendon Burchard's six Es: envision, enlist, embody, empower, evaluate, encourage?
6   The ability to empower the team?

What can you do to improve your score for each by just one? See 'What Can You Learn?' on page 12 and use the summary above to suggest ways that you can improve your leadership skills/selection of leaders.

CHAPTER 7

A World-class Culture

I often see culture in the same way that I see weather. There is never a point at which we have no weather. The only question is, what weather do we have? The same is true of culture. There will always be a culture within a team, the question is, what culture do we have? Every team has it's own distinct culture. Is it the culture that we want? Have we engineered our culture to ensure that it is one that we enjoy being a part of and one that is successful? Or has our culture become something that inhibits enjoyment and success?

The culture of an organisation has often been described using the phrase 'the way things are done around here'. It is an extension of our understanding of wider culture in society. Social culture is often thought of as the common ideas, beliefs, customs, attitudes and behaviours of a particular group of people. Within cultures, we have common ways of thinking and perceiving. We accept things, appreciate things and celebrate things, and we are repulsed by things in the same way. Our culture provides a framework to help us recognise our shared understanding of the world. Nancy Jarvis understands culture as 'the totality of what a group of people think, how they behave, and what they produce that is passed on to future generations, is what binds us together as human beings but also separates us into our different communities'.[1]

To help a corporate executive leadership team understand what culture means in their world, I explained it like this: 'Our culture is what we say and do every day.'

How do cultures develop?

Having read various theories and ideas, and spoken to people with a great deal more expertise on cultural ideas than I have, there seem to be several factors in the development of cultures. First, cultures develop through necessity. Put simply, we need a set of common understandings in order to live and work together. Imagine if we had to establish common ground with people in every new interaction. There are some things, such as our fundamental views of what's right and wrong, that we need to know we all share. We need to know that the people we're living alongside and working with also accept that murdering people is wrong and that it's not OK to steal from each other. It helps us to avoid constant conflict and establish a baseline of social harmony. It also allows us to develop rules and laws that govern our society.

In many cases, cultures are also shaped by the environment, the situation, the challenges and demands on a group of people. Many indigenous tribes lived a life that was immersed in their natural surroundings. They understood the rhythm of nature and that they needed to live symbiotically with it. Therefore, many tribal cultures were founded on celebrating and valuing the natural world. Through their spiritual beliefs, they worshipped and celebrated the wildlife and the landscape in which they lived. Tribes tended to be relatively isolated. They wouldn't have had a broad, global view of their place in the world. Therefore, their sense of being part of something bigger focused on their ancestors and the recognition that their life on earth was a moment in time. They developed dances, rituals, art, music and ceremonies that embedded these beliefs.

Our cultures will also be informed by the people within them, their vision and their influence. Some individuals have a significant impact on their culture and can actually contribute to a cultural shift. Arguably, historical figures such as Dr Martin Luther King, Nelson Mandela and Mahatma Gandhi are examples of people who helped shape the culture around them. As Nancy Jarvis emphasised, our understanding of culture is transmitted from person to person. We learn it from other people.[2] We adopt the values, beliefs and behaviours of others. Sometimes we do this actively, because we choose to. On the other hand, many sociologists would argue that much of our learning is done passively – by default. They would suggest that simply because we are immersed in our society we take on its values and copy the behaviours that we see around us in order to fit in. Like gravity, culture often exerts an invisible, yet powerful, force.

What is your team culture?

Understanding what culture is gives us a starting point. But how can we begin to understand what our own team culture is? How are things actually done around here? What do we value and believe? How can we understand and articulate our common ideas, beliefs, customs, attitudes and behaviours? What do we accept, and what don't we? How do we think, perceive, decide and act?

I've witnessed many workshop sessions in which the senior management team brainstorms those characteristics that they wish to define their culture. You might have taken part in one or two of these workshops yourself. There are often a few common themes that emerge. Many teams want a culture that:

- Is focused on excellence.

- Is built on honesty and integrity.

- Is where people go the extra mile.

- Values people and listens to them.

- Is a great place to be.

- Is driven to be the best.

- Is customer focused.

- Is innovative and creative.

- Brings out the best in everyone.

Victorious Clipper yacht skipper Brendan Hall deliberately sought to make the boat a great place to be and to create a performance-focused culture that was based on knowledge-sharing, openness and solidarity. These are all admirable qualities. I have not heard many organisations aspiring to create a culture that is dominated by corporate politics, where people are negative, self-serving and do as little as possible to get by. However, I have seen quite a few environments where these are rife.

Compare cultures

I recently noticed a marked difference between the culture that I saw in some of the most successful sports teams in the world, and a team that has arguably under-performed consistently for years.

Great cultures	Not-so-great cultures
No arrogance/ego	Arrogance, insecurity and ego-dominant
Humility and modesty	Show-boating/alpha culture
Responsibility	Blame and excuses
Beginner's mind	Know-it-all
Focused on us	Focused on me
Value performance, process and preparation	Value results
Stab me in the front	Stab you in the back

I'm sure you get the picture. It's great to have all these words on the flipchart sheet. They can certainly help us to understand the culture that we want, but they don't tell us about the culture we have. One of the executive leadership teams that I work with had a very well-defined idea of the culture that they wanted to create, so we used this to help understand the culture that they had. Quite simply, I asked which members of their team embodied the cultural values that they aspired to? Who lived them consistently through their words and actions? We drew a horizontal line on a piece of paper with a zero at one end and a ten at the other. Ten represented a 100 per cent alignment between the things that each person said and did every day and the cultural values that the business aspired to. Then, we plotted the proximity of each member of the team against that 'perfect ten'. The executive team began to see a visual representation of their actual team culture, against their desired culture. If our culture is 'what we say and do every day', the question is: what do we actually say and do every day? Or more specifically: what do your people say and do every day?

In reality, this particular leadership team had some people who were very closely aligned with the culture they desired. Fortunately, most of their people were in pretty close proximity (within a couple of points), but there were also a few outliers who tended not to display those things that the team valued. Armed with this information, they could begin to see how to evolve their team culture and create the environment they desired.

Start with great people

In the words of management guru and author Jim Collins, you need to 'get the right people on the bus'.[3] In Chapter 2, we discovered the importance of recruiting well. Recruitment decisions can have an enormous impact on the culture of an organisation. Leaders need to know the cultural influence that new recruits will have on those around them. When we understand the importance of bringing the right people into the team, we also begin to see how we can build a great culture through great people. Sir David Brailsford has lead Team Sky to successive Tour de France victories, as well as engineering the unprecedented Olympic success of British Cycling. Sir David explained that it is 'incredible what you can do with the right people when you optimise your talent in a dynamic, challenging, fun and energetic culture'. He is adamant that people create the culture. Therefore, recruitment and selection are essential to that process. Get the right people and your culture will be formed.[4]

How does this apply to you?

During Chapter 2, we reflected upon the way world-class teams understand the importance of recruiting on character and attitude. In essence, it is a simple principle and one that many leaders would endorse. Interestingly, though, there are very few organisations that actually do it in practice. When I look at the recruitment processes that most teams employ, the traditional methods of using CVs, interviews and one or two psychometrics, still prevails. As a result, most organisations still recruit on skills, knowledge, qualifications and experience – not character. I recently heard a friend of mine saying that businesses 'hire on skills and fire on attitude'. If we genuinely want to develop a great culture, we need to remember that recruiting the right people is the bedrock. Done well, it makes the rest of the process relatively easy. Professor Damian Hughes explains that Manchester United boss Sir Alex Ferguson invested time assessing character when recruiting players such as David Beckham, Ryan Giggs, Paul Scholes and Gary Neville from the academy.[5] To help do this, he would invite players into his office to review video footage of their recent performances. Importantly, Ferguson was assessing how the players evaluated their performance, whether they took responsibility and had a hunger to improve. Those who showed the right character and attitude became first-team players.

Evolve your team culture

Most leaders have already got a team in place. Although they might be able to make a few changes in personnel, clearing out and starting from scratch is probably not a realistic option, so how can we evolve our team culture? Personally, I tend to work in pictures and images. I see cultural influences like gravitational fields. Imagine two gravitational cores at opposite ends of a spectrum. One represents a positive culture and the other represents a negative culture. These two cores are groups of people that embody the two opposing cultures. Moons, planets and stars have gravitational influence over each other. In a similar way individuals and groups of people have a cultural influence over each other.

In physics, there is a relationship between the mass of an

object and its gravitational pull. I see the same in cultures. The number of people, and the strengths of the influence they exert on those around them, dictates how much pull they will have over others.

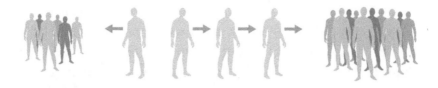

The pull of opposing cultures

Imagine your positive and negative cultural influences like gravitational cores. Which has the strongest pull?

You may see this play out in an organisation when cliques and different factions develop. You might have a group who are cultural champions. Conversely, there might also be a group of people who always seem to moan and create negativity. These groups will have the greatest influence, or gravitational pull, over those people whose mindset and values are closest to theirs. If there are people in your organisation who tend towards the negative, it is likely that they'll begin to align themselves with the group that moans and criticises. Equally, those who tend towards the positive are likely to align with the group of cultural champions.

Understanding this helps us to realise how we can evolve our team culture so that we create the environment we desire. Leaders can help to ensure that they build strength in the positive core by encouraging those people who embody a positive culture to involve and include others. This helps to translate the culture from one person to the next and extend the common understanding of what we value, how we think and what we do.

Turning the vision into reality

Many great leaders also add extra touches to help the process along. On board *Spirit of Australia*, skipper Brendan Hall was keen to encourage knowledge sharing and learning. To do this, he decided never to stifle new ideas. All ideas would be embraced and considered first, then filtered. He also presented a prize for the best trainer on each leg of the journey, to emphasise that sharing knowledge was important and valued. To embed the competitive mindset, the crew agreed not to join in with the rest of the fleet when they trash-talked opposing boats. Instead, they would keep their minds on their own jobs. They also decided to pump the bilge every half an hour, even when most boats would deem it unnecessary. This small act was a way of recognising how just reducing the weight by a few kilos helped them move the boat quicker. Each of these elements served to reinforce the crew's understanding that 'this is what we do around here'.

The value of 'normal populations'

I don't remember much of what my teachers taught me at school. It's not that I wasn't paying attention, it's just that it's a long time ago now. One thing I do remember is the concept of normal distribution in a population: the bell-shaped curve. This concept proposes that the characteristics of a population tend to collect around averages. Put simply, whichever characteristic we pick, most people will be average. There will be a few who are exceptionally good and a few who are exceptionally poor. But the majority will be neither. Instead, they'll be average. This thinking also applies to cultures. There are people who will always be fantastic, regardless of what culture they're in. Equally, there will be people who will be negative, regardless of what culture they're in. These people will not tend to change. It is more likely that if the culture does not suit them they will leave. These people are the extremes of the population, not the majority.

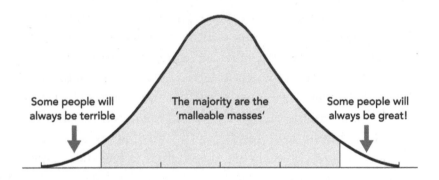

A normal distribution curve depicting a population.

In cultures, 90 per cent of people lie between the two extremes. Interestingly, these people often are more willing to change than to leave. I think of them as 'the malleable masses'. They typically prefer to belong to the crowd. They don't want to stick out or be at one of the extremes. Therefore, they tend to move towards the dominant culture. If we have two gravitational cores, the malleable masses will opt to move towards the strongest of them. Importantly, it does not mean that they move towards the positive core. Instead, they tend to move towards the one with the strongest influence: the most people and the loudest voice. When leaders are aware of this, they begin to understand the importance of deliberately increasing the strength and influence of the positive core.

When cultures melt down

In his book, *The Wisdom of Crowds*, James Surowiecki also describes the irrationality of mobs.[6] He shares an example of a mob in Seattle that baited a 26-year-old woman to jump off the Seattle Memorial Bridge in August 2001. The woman stopped her car in rush-hour traffic and climbed over the railing. Of course, a traffic jam started to develop behind her stranded vehicle and the drivers of those cars began to get angry. Rubberneckers on the other carriageway also caused a queue to form in the opposite direction. Police were called to the scene and began trying to talk the woman off the ledge. Incredibly, as they did so, angry motorists and passengers on a queuing bus began to shout, 'Get it over with!' and 'Just jump bitch, just do it!' The mob's shouts gained momentum and, despite the best efforts of the police, the woman jumped.

This is not an unusual phenomenon. Mob baiting is actually relatively common in suicide attempts. What's most interesting is that the vast majority of those who join in would not do so individually. In fact, if they were on their own and discovered someone contemplating suicide, they're more likely to try to talk them down. So, what happens to cause so many people to act in a completely different way when part of a crowd? Earlier I said that culture is like weather. Just as tornados are erratic micro-weather systems, so mobs are erratic micro-cultures. In these cases, it is likely that one or two instigators are able to spark others around them. On Seattle Memorial Bridge that August morning, people were getting increasingly frustrated. Some were clearly angry that this woman was causing a mass traffic jam. They might even have perceived that she was being selfish. On hearing someone else yell, 'Just jump!', these ordinarily good-natured people may have concluded their own anger was being validated. If one person was voicing it, maybe they would be justified in joining in. As they heard a second person shouting at the woman, it compounded their belief: perhaps everyone else thinks this woman is incredibly selfish too; what right does she have to mess up everybody's day?

Of course, with no dissenting voices opposing the instigators, the momentum builds. Very quickly, the malleable masses gravitate towards the instigators, and the mob begins to form. More people begin to shout, the intensity builds and the gravitational pull becomes greater.

As we know, cultures encapsulate the values, beliefs and behaviours of a group. On the Seattle Memorial Bridge, the cultural barometer was temporarily reset. What happened to the values that these people normally adopted? How were they changed so radically in such a short space of time? The intensity of the emotion, the anger and the way in which it was vocalised, seemed to create a new 'norm'. In that moment, the majority of rational, compassionate, everyday folk adopted the values of a minority of angry instigators, but why? As James Surowiecki explains, it is because it seemed that everyone else was doing it. The malleable masses simply followed what they perceived to be the dominant culture: the loudest voices and the strongest influence.

Influence the choices that people make

Although it might seem that the people on Seattle Memorial Bridge blindly followed the crowd, it is important to realise that our actions are always governed by choice. Sometimes we choose to follow the masses, but importantly: we choose. Cultural evolution hinges on encouraging people to choose to move towards the positive culture. In order to create the culture that we desire, people have to choose to think differently, perceive things differently, talk differently and act differently. On the basis that our culture is what we say and do every day, our people have to choose to say and do different things on a daily basis.

In the previous chapter, I shared a term with you: 'cultural architects'. This term refers to those people in the team who have significant influence over others. These are the people who drive the culture by impacting on those around them. When the leaders in an organisation can influence these cultural architects, they, in turn, have a positive impact on others. Therefore, it makes sense for leaders to know who their cultural architects are. It is also important that leaders understand why the cultural architects, and everyone else, will choose to change the things they do and say every day.

How do leaders engage these people? Here is an excerpt from a report that I wrote for a client:

If we want to create a cultural shift, we need to ensure that everyone understands why the values we're adopting are important. Why is it important to arrive at 8.27am and not 8.33am? You'll say it's to be at the team meeting on time. Why are the team meetings important? How can we ensure that they are always of value and that people don't want to be late? It makes sense to create a golden rule for the meetings, which simply states that those 15 minutes need to be really valuable. What would happen if we made the meetings unmissable?

Understand why these things are important for the team, not just for you! These things are important to the team because ...?

Remember, people choose to either move towards, or

away from, your ideal culture. How can you influence them to move towards the ideal?

People are motivated in different ways. One of the strongest motivators for some people is a need to belong and not get left out. Although it sounds 'soft', for some people the need to belong will always trump hard motivators such as money.

Create something to be proud of

Several years ago I worked with an organisation called the English Institute of Sport (EIS). Our job, very simply, was to provide sport science support to the Team GB Olympic programmes and England teams. I joined the EIS in 2004, shortly after it was formed. At that time we were following in the footsteps of the well-established Australian Institute of Sport (AIS) and US Olympic programme (USOC). We often looked upon the AIS and USOC as the leaders in the field. They were our examples of best practice and provided a benchmark for us. However, in the lead-up to the Beijing Olympic Games of 2008, we began to realise that our processes at the EIS were probably better than those of our competition. When we looked at the quality of practice around the world, we became aware that we were no longer following – we had become the world leaders.

This realisation sparked an interesting transformation. As a practitioner, I began to feel real pride in the team. Whenever I pulled on my uniform – the black shirt and tracksuit – I was reminded that I belonged to a truly elite organisation. My respect for my team members, and the work that we all did, grew as a consequence. Although at that point we didn't have the results to prove it, we were aware that our team was world class. In 2008, the Team GB medal haul provided the validation.

Importantly, the pride came first – born out of our belief in our processes – and the results followed.

This method applies outside Olympic sports. I have used exactly the same principles with many businesses and sports teams. It starts by focusing on delivering world-class processes. When they understand that what they do every day is truly excellent, the team begin to develop pride in it. When team members understand that they are all excelling in their field, they also deepen their respect for each other. Of course, the formula is simple, but that doesn't mean it's easy!

In Chapter 2 we looked at organisations that have become a magnet for talent. Often, it is because they are recognised as being the very best at what they do. Many people aspire to be part of something special. We often feel a vicarious sense of self-pride simply by belonging to a team that is elite. In many cases, teams that are at the very pinnacle of the world create a tangible way to recognise those who pass their tests and join their ranks. The Royal Marines are known to have the longest, and one of the toughest, military training programmes in the world. When their recruits pass-out, they are awarded the legendary Green Beret. The Green Beret becomes more than just a hat. It means that you've got what it takes to be a Royal Marine Commando. You have endured the hardship, pushed yourself to the limits and passed the toughest of tests. Importantly, you know that you have earned the right! It is because you had to work for it that it feels special. With that comes a great deal of pride in yourself and recognition that the organisation you've joined is special. Everyone else around you earned their right to be there too. Many sports teams adopt a similar approach when awarding shirts to their players. The British and Irish Lions traditionally present shirts to players at an informal award ceremony. They're congratulating the players on joining an elite and special group. It is an honour for any player to represent their country. When four countries join together, only the very best of the best will become 'a Lion'. This simple act is also used in business. One of my corporate clients awards 'Master' status to its elite engineers to recognise them as the very best in their industry.

Reinventing a team culture – the All Blacks

James Kerr is a New Zealander who spent five weeks in camp with the All Blacks. James is not an athlete, a sports coach or a sport psychologist. Other than being a proud New Zealander, his interest in the All Blacks is not sporting – it's cultural. In his professional life, James helps organisations to define, design and deliver cultural-change programmes. During his five weeks with the All Blacks, he studied their culture and, perhaps more interestingly, how they created it. I had the enormous pleasure of co-delivering an event called, 'On ... All Black Culture', in which James shared his insights.[7]

Although we might think of the All Blacks as a team that has enjoyed wall-to-wall success, the reality is different. At the turn of the millennium, they were struggling. It came to a head in 2004 when they lost the Tri-Nations series in South Africa. Not only were they losing on the field but they were also in real trouble internally. The culture was described as 'drink or sink'. It was a highly dysfunctional, uber-macho, alcohol-fuelled alpha culture, which a lot of players simply didn't want to be a part of. The coaching team knew they needed to turn it around – and fast.

Their process was one that combined reinvention with rediscovery. The All Blacks leadership did not only look forward and envision a culture that they desired, they also looked back as well. To reinvent the culture, they embraced the changes that were happening in society and in the game of rugby. New Zealand was becoming more multicultural. There was greater integration of the white European, Maori and Pacific Island cultures. The game of rugby was also moving from an amateur era into a professional era. As well as looking forward, the All Blacks leadership was also acutely aware of the need to create an authentic culture; one that was grounded in the traditions of the All Blacks as well as the Kiwi and Maori peoples.

To do this, they began to ask what it meant to be an All Black, a New Zealander and a man. What does it mean to be alive? To understand their collective identity, they asked: 'Who are we?' and 'What do we stand for?' Personal authenticity stems from self-knowledge. We have to know who we are in order to be ourselves. The same is true collectively. To be true to ourselves, we must first know ourselves. We must understand our collective identity. The All Blacks leadership team also had personal conversations with the players and staff to ensure that they aligned personal purpose with public meaning. It ensures that each person had a clear sense of *who I am* in relation to the team.

Therefore, the culture that they built had a very strong and shared sense of *why?*. In doing so, they re-established meaning. One example of this is the way they reconnected with the haka (a traditional Maori war dance that the All Blacks perform before each game). In James Kerr's words, it had started to lose its meaning and had become more of a tourist war dance and a branding tool. The All Blacks invested a great deal of focus into making the haka their own again and knowing what it stands for.

As with many great cultures, the All Blacks recognise their higher purpose. Theirs revolves around the desire to leave a legacy. They appreciate that there were many who came before them, and there will be many that follow. As current All Blacks, each player is a part of this relatively small moment in time. Therefore, players have a responsibility to be the custodian of their shirt. In their words, they seek 'to leave the shirt in a better place'. They live this principle by aiming to be a great All Black. It is their way of living an even higher principle – to be a great ancestor. It is not enough to simply pull the shirt on. What you do while you've got it is key. Of course, being a great All Black requires you to strive for excellence every day, not just on game day. It requires you to do things and say things that will enable you to be the best you can possibly be and to constantly look for ways to become ever better.

As with many cultures, the All Blacks have found ways to live their values. In some cases they deliberately ritualise these. One such example is the way they 'sweep the sheds'. In James Kerr's words, 'Humility is one of their cardinal values.' They have decided that no one looks after the All Blacks; the All Blacks look after themselves. No All Black is too big to do the little things. Nothing is beyond us, and we don't get ahead of ourselves. Therefore, after every game, the players pick up long-handled brooms and begin to clean the dressing room. Through this simple act, they are turning a value into a behaviour. This is just one example of many values that the All Blacks live by. Of course, there are many more, from adopting a beginner's mind, to the value of 'stabbing each other in the front' (having the brutal honesty to tell each other what they really think) and the wider understanding that great people make great All Blacks. With these foundations, they emphasise the need to recruit on character not skills and develop character in people as well as skills in players.

In closing the event with James Kerr, I reflected on a simple turn of phrase that illustrates the power of the All Black culture. We refer to *'playing* for England' and *'being* an All Black'.

The principle works in other organisations too

Obviously, a world-class culture is not exclusive to the All Blacks. Equally, you could not cut and paste the All Blacks culture into another organisation and expect success. It is uniquely theirs; bespoke, authentic and built to fit. Of course, the principles that the All Blacks employed can be seen in many other environments. To be honest, the 'secret formula' is not revolutionary. When I look at the ingredients of a world-class culture, I simply see the best of humanity. I see people who know themselves and are happy to be themselves. I see those who are dedicated to a higher purpose. I see people who are self-less. I see humility.

Sir Ian McGeechan coached the victorious British and Irish Lions team that toured South Africa in 1997. He reflected on the challenges that accompany a touring squad. There are 37 players on the tour, and only 15 starting places available in the Test team. Therefore, dealing with the disappointment of being left out of the side is critical to the harmony of the squad and the chances of success in the Test matches. Sir Ian is convinced it is those players who aren't selected that determine the environment.

> I will forever say that Jason Leonard was one of the best Lions I have ever come across because of what he did in 1997 to make sure the two props (who were selected for the Tests) were ready to go in and do a job. It's the midweek team that sets the environment and if the environment is right, the Test team will be right.[8]

Andy Walshe, high-performance director at Team Red Bull, says that their environment works because they have a clear, concise understanding of their vision. They know how they all want to be represented as a human. Everyone understands 'the non-negotiables'. Whenever there is disagreement, they go back to these fundamental principles.[9]

Each of the teams that I have studied has an acute awareness of the fundamental elements that drive their culture. Of course, there are different contexts and demands upon them. They have different challenges and aims. However, they have all created a strong and distinct culture. These teams also find simple, clear ways of communicating it. They create rituals that turn values into behaviours. This allows their people to understand and adopt the collective ways of thinking and being.

How does this apply to you

How can you begin to ensure that cultural ideas and values become a part of what people actually say and do every day? How can you change the thought processes and conversations? What meaningful rituals would turn your cultural ideals into behaviours?

How strong is the culture?

Cultures get tested. Fundamentally, cultures express our collective values. Life continually presents us with challenges that test our values. Individually, we make decisions that are either aligned with our values or that compromise them. Most people will say that honesty is a core value. However, those same people will occasionally tell little white lies. The question is, when does a little white lie become dishonesty? Those who will say that they value honesty might also hide inconvenient truths, exaggerate accounts or decide to cover up embarrassing moments by flexing the truth.

The test of values extends beyond an individual to teams and organisations. Brendan Hall explained that there were some simple overriding philosophies that guided the way they worked and made decisions.[10] One of their guiding principles was that they focus on 'long term victory not short term glory'. This underpinned their decisions to take either the higher-risk option and push the boat to its limit or adopt a more conservative, low-risk approach. According to this philosophy, the crew of *Spirit of Australia* would reduce their sails in high winds, choosing smaller, tougher sails that put less strain on ropes and masts. They knew that there was a trade-off between bigger sails that increased speed and the risk of damage and injury that came with them.

Brendan found that having a philosophy was one thing, but abiding by it when you're behind and chasing your opponent, is another. On one occasion, while crossing the Southern Ocean, he pushed the boat too hard in an attempt to chase down the leader. The result was a high-speed crash in treacherous conditions, which caused damage to the boat, injury to crew members and inevitably slowed them down. There is obviously a negative impact on race position and performance. More significantly, when people see the leader making a decision that contradicts their stated values, it is likely to compromise the culture.

How does this apply to you?

I have spoken to many employees who are perplexed as they walk into their office. They see the big colourful signage as they walk in, stating the company's mission, its values and its promises. Then they reflect on the decisions that are made on a daily basis and the way that staff and customers are treated. There seems to be a gulf between the words on the wall and the world they experience. Cultures are not just tested by monumental events. They are tested on a moment-by-moment basis, in every decision, conversation and action. How do we discipline people? Are we really honest? Do we really treat people with respect? Do we genuinely empower our people, value them and seek to get the best from them? When it looks like we might miss our target, do we opt for profit and sacrifice quality? Do we allow people to make mistakes and learn, or do we always push for the result? Do we genuinely look to learn from mistakes or criticise those who make them? Are those words on the signage really the values by which we live, or are they just words?

Sir Alex Ferguson managed Manchester United from 1986 to 2013. One thing that Ferguson always maintained is that no player is bigger than the club. During his tenure, he signed a number of superstar players. He also brought groups of talented young players, such as David Beckham, through the Academy into the professional ranks. Regularly, Sir Alex's philosophy was challenged by the team's star player. Would he bend to the will of the player and, in doing so, compromise the culture? Or would he risk losing his best player, and possibly risk losing games, in order to protect the culture? His answer, consistently, was to lose the player and preserve the culture. It is a challenge that many managers face: 'What do I do with my high performer who detracts from the culture?'

Our culture is what we say and do every day – not, what we say that we say and do.

Summary

There will always be a culture in our team. The question is: what will our culture be? Is it the one that we want? Is it the one that we have engineered? What are our common ideas, values, beliefs and behaviours? Most teams aspire to have a positive culture, but there are relatively few that succeed. World-class teams understand that recruiting and selecting the right people is the foundation. To evolve our existing culture, we need to understand how people influence each other and who our cultural architects are. People choose whether to adopt values and behaviours. Understanding why people make these choices is crucial. Cultures live only when people live the values. Developing meaningful rituals helped the All Blacks turn values into behaviours. Of course, as more people begin to do great things and say great things on a daily basis, the culture begins to shift.

- Understand your team culture. Understand what it is, what its values are, and how your common ideas and beliefs are articulated. Identify the qualities that you want your culture to embody. Bridge the gap between the words on the flipchart sheet and the things people say and do every day.

- Recruiting well is essential. Understand the cultural influence that new recruits will have on the existing culture of the team and recruit wisely.

- To help your team evolve positively, recognise that the number of people, and the strength of the influence they exert on those around them, dictates how much pull they will have over others, whether that is positive or negative. Build strength in the positive core by encouraging those people who embody a positive culture to involve and include others.

- In order to create the culture that you desire, people will have to choose to think differently, perceive things differently, talk differently and act differently. Influence the cultural architects – those who have significant influence over others – to create a positive influence on others.

- Create something that the team can be proud of – something that will be a magnet for talent. When team members understand that what they do every day is truly excellent, they will begin to develop real pride in it.

- A world-class team culture has people who are selfless and are happy to be themselves and are dedicated to a higher purpose.

WORKSHOP: World-class culture

Reflect on what you see as your team culture at the moment. Take a moment and score your team using the simple 0–10 scale. As before, a score of 10 means 'perfect, flawless, cannot be improved'. A score of zero means that there is nothing good about it.

Do you have:

1 A clear vision of the culture you wish to create?
2 An accurate assessment of the culture you currently have?
3 The ability to get the right people on the bus?
4 Strength and influence over your positive core?
5 Knowledge of your cultural architects and their strength of influence?
6 Alignment between public purpose and private meaning?

What can you do to improve your score for each by just one? See 'What Can You Learn?' on page 12 and use the summary above to suggest ways that you can improve the way your team culture evolves.

CHAPTER 8

Developing World-class Teamwork

I am a great fan of keeping things simple. Whenever I have a complex task, I often start by trying to simplify it. Developing world-class teamwork might seem complicated at first. So far we've shared about 50,000 words on the topic, so putting all these ideas into action could seem a little daunting. This feeling is often exacerbated if we look at our own team and conclude that there's a considerable gap between it and a 'world-class' team, so where do we start? Have you come across the 'Plan – Do – Review' cycle? I've seen a few variations on this over the years, but the base principle tends to be the same. The name 'Plan – Do – Review' suggests that the process starts with planning, but I'm not so sure.

Personally, I believe that the start of the process is to review. I'd argue that without a review, we can't really create a sensible plan. The plan needs to be informed by something, so it makes sense to figure out where we are before deciding upon where we need to go. Reviewing helps us to know where we are.

Review

You will already have seen the workshop sections at the end of each chapter, which ask you to reflect on your team and how it can be improved. The questions are designed to stimulate your thinking, help you assess your team and therefore inform your plan. These questions are a great starting point. By scoring yourself on a 0–10 scale (where 10 is 'perfect, flawless and cannot be improved' and zero means 'there is nothing good about it') we begin to see our relative strengths and weaknesses. It also allows us to identify priority areas to work on and therefore helps us to refine our focus.

You'll find some additional questions in this chapter. These are designed to help stimulate your thinking, probe a little deeper, go beyond the headlines and get under the skin of the issues. For example, to help us understand whether our team really is *highly focused*, these follow-up questions ask whether we have a strong, clear and shared purpose. Do we all know our *why?* The questions also ask whether we know our 'two lengths of the pool' (our job in the simplest possible terms) and our 'five keys' (the really important processes we need to deliver). Therefore, these additional questions help us to refine our thinking so that we can score ourselves accurately and also understand how to develop our team in each area.

THE CHARACTERISTICS OF WORLD-CLASS TEAMS (CHAPTER 1)

How does your team rate against the six characteristics?

1 Highly focused

2 Shared standards and expectations

3 Total appreciation of each individual

4 Draw strength from their differences

5 Brutal honesty

6 Always learning

Score from 0–10.   ▶

To help answer these, you could also ask some follow-up questions:

1 Do we have a shared 'why?'

2 Do we all understand our 'two lengths of the pool' and our 'five keys'?

3 Do we understand what 'good enough' looks like, sounds like and behaves like?

4 Do we understand and recognise the value in everyone's contribution?

5 How well do we understand the personalities within the team and how to get the best from each other?

6 When do people really say what they think and feel? When is there a gap between what people should say and what they do say?

7 How good are you at collectively learning from your experiences and constantly improving?

What can you now do to improve your score for each by just one?

RECRUITMENT AND SELECTION (CHAPTER 2)

How well do you apply the following elements?

1 Do you know what the 'perfect person'
   looks like?   ☐

2 Do you test potential recruits?   ☐

3 How well do you deal with the situation
   if you recruited the wrong person?   ☐

4 Is your team a magnet for talent?   ☐

5 Do you select balanced teams?   ☐

6 Are the teams you select well matched
   to the challenge?   ☐

7 Do you create continuity through
   selection?   ☐

Score from 0–10.

To help answer these, you could also ask some follow-up
questions:

1 Do you have a clear idea of what the ideal recruit looks like
   in terms of attitude, character, personality and mentality?

2 How can you test for this?

3 Does your recruitment process extend beyond CVs,
   interviews and psychometric tests?

4 Do you use the probation period to find out whether the
   person you've recruited is genuinely a good fit? Do you

▶

deselect people if they don't fit? Or is your probation period merely a formality?

5 When do you identify whether a new recruit is likely to be right? If there is a doubt, when and how do you act?

6 How do you understand whether your new recruit is a good team player?

7 Why do people want to join your team?

8 Why would the very best of the best want to join your team?

9 How can we make sure that we recruit and select square pegs for square holes and give them the best chance of succeeding?

10 How well balanced are the teams that we select?

11 How well do we create continuity, and help teams learn how to work well together?

What can you now do to improve your score for each by just one?

GREAT TEAM PLAYERS (CHAPTER 3)

How willing are your people to:

1 Take responsibility?

2 Align to team goals?

▶

3 Ask for help when they need it and allow
others to 'carry their bag'?

4 Put the team before the needs of their
own ego?

5 Play *for* the team, rather than just *in* the team?

Score from 0–10.

To help answer these, you could also ask some follow-up
questions:

1 Who is happy to ask for help when they need it?

2 Who is more interested in looking good, or avoiding
looking bad, as an individual?

3 Who opts to blame rather than taking responsibility?

4 Who is selfless and focuses on the team?

5 Who plays *for* the team, and who plays *in* the team?

6 What do you see in those who play *for* the team, not just
in the team?

What can you now do to improve your score for each by just
one?

WORLD-CLASS TEAMWORK (CHAPTER 4)

How well do you:

1 Understand the need to work together
   as a team?

2 Collectively respond to changes in your
   environment?

3 Recognise inter-dependencies?

4 Ensure that everyone knows their job and
   is held accountable for delivery?

5 Adopt 'less is more' communication?

6 Collectively solve problems?

Score from 0–10.

To help answer these, you could also ask some follow-up
questions:

1 How strong is your rationale for working together?

2 Do you all understand the reason for your team in the
   same way?

3 Do your team members all recognise the need to invest in
   their relationships with each other?

4 Do you have clear SOPs and ways of working that
   everyone understands in the same way?

5 Does your team have a shared understanding of how to

▶

detect and communicate changes in your environment and how to respond to them?

6 What is your *why?*, *what?*, *when?*, *who?* and *how?* of communication?

7 Do your team members inhibit, allow or enable each other's performance?

8 Do your team members understand how they are dependent on each other and how their actions affect those around them?

9 When do you collectively solve problems? How effective are you?

What can you now do to improve your score for each by just one?

IMPROVING TEAM PERFORMANCE (CHAPTER 5)

How would you rate:

1 Your compelling reason to improve all the time?

2 Your ability to improve the performance of individuals?

3 Your ability to raise standards, not just targets?

4 Clarity created through briefings with a focus on processes?

▶

5 The quality of your practise and debrief?   [   ]

Score from 0–10.

To help answer these, you could also ask some follow-up questions:

1 Does everyone understand and share the compelling reason to constantly improve?

2 Does your team's performance dip when you hit a danger zone?

3 Does your team tend to dedicate more focus to improvement when things go wrong?

3 Are your people consistently focused, confident and motivated?

4 Do they know their job simply and clearly?

5 Do your people focus on delivering the processes or on the outcome?

6 Do you focus on raising standards or increasing targets?

7 How well do you plan, prepare and practise?

8 How well do you debrief?

9 Do you drive performance by asking great questions?

10 How much fun do you have?

What can you now do to improve your score for each by just one?

WORLD-CLASS LEADERSHIP (CHAPTER 6)

How would you rate:

1 The depth of leadership? ⬚

2 The ability to switch leaders and adopt
   fluid leadership? ⬚

3 The balance of your leadership team? ⬚

4 Your leaders' strength of influence? ⬚

5 Your leadership, using Brendon Burchard's
   six E's: envision, enlist, embody, empower,
   evaluate, encourage? ⬚

6 The ability to empower the team? ⬚

Score from 0–10.

To help answer these, you could also ask some follow-up
questions:

1 Is your team reliant on a single individual, or do you
   have a team of leaders?

2 How great is the depth of leadership in your team?

3 Where could you become more effective by switching the
   leadership to those with specific situational experience or
   expertise?

4 How balanced and well-rounded is your leadership team?

5 Who are the cultural architects in your team? Who has
   the greatest influence on those around them?

▶

6 Why do your people follow you? Why do they follow the leaders within your organisation?

7 Do your leaders empower their teams?

8 How many of the characteristics of world-class leaders do you see in yourself?

9 How well developed are these characteristics in your leaders?

10 What do you need to develop in order to move towards world-class leadership?

11 What is the next logical step in this journey?

What can you now do to improve your score for each by just one?

WORLD-CLASS CULTURE (CHAPTER 7)

Do you have:

1 A clear vision of the culture you wish to create?

2 An accurate assessment of the culture you currently have?

3 The ability to get the right people on the bus?

4 Strength and influence over your positive core?

▶

5 Knowledge of your 'cultural architects' and their strength of influence?

6 Alignment between public purpose and private meaning?

Score from 0–10.

To help answer these, you could also ask some follow-up questions:

1 What culture do you aspire to create?

2 What culture do you currently have? What do your people say and do on a daily basis?

3 Why will they choose to adopt the culture that you desire?

4 How can you instil pride in your team and make it something that your people want to belong to?

5 Who are your cultural architects?

6 How can you help your team to live the values?

7 How can you develop meaningful rituals that turn values into behaviours?

8 What happens when your values get tested? Are your decisions completely aligned with your values, or do you compromise them?

What can you now do to improve your score for each by just one?

Plan

A strong review informs and lays the foundations for a strong plan. Once we know where we are, we can begin to plot a course for our desired destination, but where do you start? I often advocate beginning with those things that are the highest priority. By that, I mean the areas that will have the most significant impact on our performance. To be more specific, I suggest focusing on the areas that will help us to swim our two lengths of the pool as quickly as possible. The Red Arrows often talk about making 'mission centric' decisions: 'What will help us to achieve the mission?' I often work with performance directors of Olympic Programmes. Their aim, very simply, is to secure as many Olympic medals as possible – preferably gold ones. One of their challenges is to understand how to allocate their budget. There are hundreds of things they could spend it on. Do they spend money on equipment, training camps, travelling to competitions or more support staff? Which of these things will bring medals? Importantly, the Performance Director needs to understand how cash translates to performance. To help, I often ask a simple question: 'Regardless of how much or how little it costs, if you could only do one thing, what would it be? Which is the one thing you wouldn't do without? You can only have one!' Once we know what that one thing is, we repeat the process a second time, then a third time, and so on until the budget is allocated. The same discipline can be applied to any other resource, including time and focus. This thought process helps to establish the priorities.

Identify priorities, then improve performance

Once we know the priorities, we can start working out how to improve the performance in those areas. I like to start by looking at the score for each. The review exercise asks for a score out of 10. The score that you give will tend to represent an average. For example, you may have scored yourself a 6 out of 10 for a particular area. Inevitably there will be times when you're better than a 6. Equally, there will probably be times when you're not quite as good as a 6. With each of your scores, ask yourself: 'At our best, how good are we? How high do we score on a great day? Equally, when we're not on form, how low would we score?' Once you know the range, you can start to identify what you're like on your best days. What do your best days look like? What do you do differently on your best days? Many people imagine that to improve their performance they need to do something differently. I believe that we can improve simply by doing what we do at our best, more regularly. How much better would you be if you were able to replicate your best day every day?

It is often extremely beneficial to understand the tangible difference between where you are right now and a score just one point higher. If you have scored yourself at 6 out of 10, what will be different when you're a 7? Simply knowing the difference between a 6 and a 7 helps you to understand what you need to do to perform at a 7.

Involve the team

With this knowledge, we can begin to create a strategy to develop better teamwork. Many of the world-class leaders who have contributed to this book advocate engaging the team at this stage. Former SAS major Floyd Woodrow often talks of co-creating the plan with the team, rather than deciding upon it and then announcing it. For many leaders, this is a critical step in empowering the team to deliver. I often ask who else's input would be valuable? Who else can help us make the changes and implement the strategy? Which partners do we need to engage with? I also like to know how we'll assess our progress. How will we know that we're improving? What will we see and hear differently? Are there any metrics that we can use?

Once we have this outline plan, we can begin to stress test it for robustness. We can challenge it and begin to ask some of the 'what if?' questions. Most teams and leaders know that invariably the *what if?* scenarios never happen in the same way that we imagine them. However, the process of asking the questions, and thinking through the response, is innately valuable. As Dwight D. Eisenhower said, 'In preparing for battle I have always found that plans are useless, but planning is indispensable.'

When developing great teamwork, often these *what if?* questions revolve around people's responses to challenges. What if those people don't want to change? What if they don't engage with the process? What if we get resistance? What if they show signs of apathy? Who is likely to respond negatively and what do we do if that's the case?

With these basic building blocks in place, we can start to pull together a plan and share it with others.

Do

The plan is in place. It's been stress-tested and endorsed by the team. You're ready to put it into action. When most people start off on a journey they are full of positive energy, confident in their plan and enthused by their new ideas. For some, this can wane slightly as they encounter challenges. I suspect it is often wise to start out expecting that the ride will not be entirely smooth. Developing a strong team requires people to change. In reality, many people don't like change, especially when it means that they need to do the changing.

Change tends to be stressful and challenging. Changes bring with them unpredictability, uncertainty and discomfort for many. The status quo, although it might be flawed and ineffective, sometimes seems more comfortable. Change is often effortful and demands more from us. It's not surprising then that organisations often find it difficult to galvanise their teams to engage with change. I'm sure you'll recognise the narratives:

Leader says, 'We need to change!'

Team member thinks, *I'm not sure I fancy that. I'm pretty comfortable where I am, thank you.*

Leader says, 'We need *you* to change!'

Team member thinks, *I wonder if I could make all the right noises but actually do nothing different?*

When faced with this challenge, I often ask, 'Why would the person choose to change? What's the reason? How will it benefit them?' As I mentioned earlier, I recently wrote a little book called *How to Herd Cats: Leading a Team of Independent Thinkers*. It asks how leaders can galvanise a team of people who all have their own egos, agendas, opinions and self-interest. From my studies of animal teams, I began to realise some fundamental truths about leadership and teamwork, which help to answer this question. For example, people tend to make independent decisions that are in their own self-interest. Crucially, these independent decisions do not have to be different. Often people independently choose to make the same decision and move in the same direction because it serves them. Therefore, it is incredibly beneficial for leaders to understand why people would choose to change.

Aim for openness

Creating the plan together, as a team, often helps people to engage with it. As humans, we tend to feel a sense of ownership when we have invested into something. However, even when we have co-created the plan and engaged the team initially we could still face these challenges along the way. Sometimes people say yes because they don't really know what changing involves.

When they actually begin to understand what's required, those who initially said yes may begin to think, *This is harder than I expected. I didn't think it would be like this. I'm not sure I like it.* When people find themselves in this position, it is pretty common for them to try to validate these thoughts. Often they'll test the water by asking whether those around them feel the same way. Mutterings might begin in the background: 'Is it just me? Are you enjoying this? Is it what you expected? What do you make of all this then?' If people find others who seem to agree with them, cliques might start to form. More people and more voices increase the strength of this negative cultural gravitational core. Gradually, there is a force that begins to resist the changes.

These are the daily challenges that leaders face when attempting to instigate change in people, teams and organisations. SAS major Floyd Woodrow explained that the same issues arise in SAS units. His story of Delta Eight and Delta Nine (in Chapter 6) highlights a very similar challenge. Importantly, Delta Nine's leader, Jim, had opportunities to diffuse the issue at an early stage but chose not to. He could have asked for honest feedback before his team members began to ask questions of themselves and of each other. Equally, when he first became aware of background mutterings, resistance or apathy, he could have chosen to engage it. Often we can detect when people are disengaged. They might not look us in the eye but choose to stare at the floor. They might avoid deeper conversations when it looks like they could become uncomfortable. Delta Nine's leader, Jim, chose not to act when he noticed these signs.

Floyd also advocates that leaders encourage open discussions on the issues at an early stage. When issues are out in the open, we can deal with them. When they're left to fester in the background, it is much harder. The challenge for the leader often is that it can involve confrontation and tough questions. Normally, it demands more from us. Thinking can be tiring and time-consuming. Sometimes the leader feels criticism and experiences a little ego-bruising along the way. As uncomfortable as it might be, these are the very real challenges that leaders will inevitably face when driving change.

A tight cycle

World-class teams are fantastic at learning from their experiences and adapting to new challenges. They are often able to do this because they adopt a very tight 'Plan – Do – Review' cycle. They quickly understand what is working and what needs tweaking. And, of course, they ensure that they make the necessary changes as they go. Leaders often require a regular, healthy dose of honest self-reflection. The American author, salesman and motivational speaker Hilary Hinton known as 'Zig' Ziglar, said, 'People often say that motivation doesn't last. Well, neither does bathing – that's why we recommend it daily.' I would argue that the same is true of self-reflection. If we only reflected every few weeks, I also suspect we'd miss some really powerful opportunities to improve. The gradient of our progression curve is often directly related to the frequency, honesty and detail of our review. Therefore, our success in developing world-class teamwork is also likely to hinge on our ability to self-reflect and adapt.

As with all things, it is easier said than done. Developing a strong team is not something that can be done with the click of a finger. It is a process that requires us to learn. Learning takes time. Inevitably we make mistakes. When we learned to walk we fell over – a lot! Importantly though, we didn't view falling over as a failure. We didn't get upset and conclude that it was too difficult, and give up. The truth is that giving up is not the *result* of failure – it is the *cause*. If you ever watch babies learning to walk, you'll notice that they employ a very simple process. If at first you don't succeed, change, then try again ... then change and try again ... If, as adults, we employed this very simple mind-set, we'd be amazed at what we could achieve.

Final words

As we know, a team can be incredibly powerful when it works. In many cases, the ability to work together and become a strong team creates a distinct competitive advantage. In truth, there aren't too many great teams out there. Strong teams are often capable of eclipsing other teams that are collections of superstar individuals who seem unable to work together. Their ability to consistently take on challenges and be successful also creates a collective confidence, which propels the team on to ever-greater achievements. Therefore, leaders who are able to create strong teams and enable great teamwork will always be sought after.

Using the insights from world-class teams, you can now begin to develop your team's ability to work together. They show us not only what makes them great, but also how they have done it. Adopting these principles can help us to get the most out of our people and help the team to perform at its best consistently. Using the very simple processes that they employ, we can also build a team with an intense sense of loyalty and a telepathic understanding. None of these qualities are mythical and they don't appear by chance. World-class teams deliberately develop these qualities using simple, tangible strategies. And by adopting the same principles, you can do the same.

I'd like to leave you with a simple thought:

> On its own, a snowflake, water droplet or ice crystal
> has little effect on the world.
> Together they shape the earth. It's the same
> with people.

References

Introduction

1. Pennington, J., 'Cricket World's 2014 predictions', *Cricket World*, 3 January 2014
2. Jones, A., Richard, B., Paul, D., Sloane K. and Peter, F., 'Effectiveness of teambuilding in organization', *Journal of Management*, 5(3) (2007), pp. 35–7
3. Hackman, J.R. and Coutu, D., 'Why teams don't work', *Harvard Business Review*, May 2009. Available online, http://hbr.org/2009/05/why-teams-dont-work/ar/1 (accessed 2 July 2014)
4. Muffett, T., 'Red Arrows celebrate their 50th display season', BBC News UK, 26 June 2014
5. Warren, J., 'Is the SAS still the world's finest elite force?', *Daily Express*, 8 March 2011. Available online, http://www.express.co.uk/expressyourself/233218/Is-the-SAS-still-the-world-s-finest-elite-force
6. Tu, K., *Superteams*, Portfolio Penguin, London (2012)
7. Woodward, C., *Winning!*, Hodder and Stoughton, London (2004)
8. Kerr, J., *Legacy*, Constable and Robinson, London (2013)

Chapter 1

1. Sinek, S., *Start With Why*, Portfolio Penguin, London (2011)
2. Ibid
3. Kerr, J., *Legacy*, Constable and Robinson, London (2013)
4. Wagman, R., Nunes, D., Burrass, J. and Hackman, J., *Senior Leadership Teams: What it Takes to Make Them Great*, Harvard Business Press, Harvard, CT (2008)
5. Hartley, S.R., *Two Lengths of the Pool: Sometimes the Simplest Ideas*

Have the Greatest Impact, Be World Class, Arkendale, UK (2013)

6. Hunt-Davis, B. and Beveridge, H., *Will it Make the Boat Go Faster?: Olympic Strategies for Everyday Success*, Matador, London (2011)

7. Hall, B., *Team Spirit*, Adlard Coles Nautical, London (2012)

8. Tu, K., *Superteams*, Portfolio Penguin, London (2012)

9. Trimble, V., *Overnight Success: FedEx and Frederick Smith, Its Renegade Creator*, Crown, New York (1993)

10. Tu, K., *Superteams*, Portfolio Penguin, London (2012)

11. Hall, B., *Team Spirit*, Adlard Coles Nautical, London (2012)

12. Jung, C.G., *Psychological Types* (*The Collected Works of C.G. Jung*, Vol. 6), Princeton University Press, Princeton, NJ (1976)

13. Brailsford, D., 'Wiggins and Froome can team up again, says Team Sky boss', BBC Sport, 23 July 2013. Available online, http://www.bbc.co.uk/sport/0/cycling/23415146

14. Weiner, N., *Cybernetics: Or Control and Communication in the Animal and the Machine*, Wiley and Sons, New York (1947)

15. Ibid

Chapter 2

1. Woodward, C., *Winning!*, Hodder and Stoughton, London (2004)

2. Tu, K., *Superteams*, Portfolio Penguin, London (2012)

3. Donegan, L., 'Colin Montgomerie's Ryder Cup wild card picks spark controversy', *Guardian*, 30 August 2010

4. Woodward, C., *Winning!*, Hodder and Stoughton, London (2004)

5. Devaney, J., *Bart Starr*, Scholastic Book Services, New York (1967)

6. McWhorter, L.V., *Yellow Wolf: His Own Story*, Caxton Press, Caldwell, Idaho (1940)

7. BBC News, 'Soldier deaths: Third SAS training reservist dies', BBC News online, 31 July 2013. Available online, http://www.bbc.co.uk/news/uk-wales-23511938 (accessed 4 July 2014)

8. Woodward, C., *Winning!*, Hodder and Stoughton, London (2004)

9. Ibid

10. Bartle, C. and Hartley, S.R., 'On ... World Class Performance. Be World Class TV', (2013). Available online. www.be-world-class.com

11. Jung, C.G., *Psychological Types* (*The Collected Works of C.G. Jung*, Vol. 6), Princeton University Press, Princeton, NJ (1976)

Chapter 3

1. Reference Dictionary (2014), accessed online 5 August 2014, http://dictionary.reference.com/browse/ego
2. Jones, C., 'British and Irish Lions; Sir Ian McGeechan – How to win a test series', BBC Sport 2013
3. Schofield, D., 'How New Zealand assistant coach Gilbert Enoka turned All Blacks around with a strict no-d***heads policy', *Daily Telegraph*, 5 November 2014. Available online, http://www.telegraph.co.uk/sport/rugbyunion/international/newzealand/11208617/How-New-Zealand-assistant-coach-Gilbert-Enoka-turned-All-Blacks-around-with-a-strict-no-dheads-policy.html (accessed 5 November 2014)
4. Jauncey, P., *Managing Yourself and Others*, CopyRight Publishing, Brisbane (2002)
5. Jackson, P., *Sacred Hoops: Spiritual Lessons of a Hardwood Warrior*, Hyperion, New York (1995), (reissued 2006)

Chapter 4

1. Woodward, C., *Winning!*, Hodder and Stoughton, London (2004)
2. Hall, B., *Team Spirit*, Adlard Coles Nautical, London (2012)
3. Jackson, P., *Sacred Hoops: Spiritual Lessons of a Hardwood Warrior*, Hyperion, New York (1995), (reissued 2006)
4. Fong, K., in *Horizon*, 'How to avoid mistakes in surgery', BBC2, first broadcast 21 March 2013
5. Goldman, A., in *Horizon*, 'How to avoid mistakes in surgery', BBC2, first broadcast 21 March 2013
6. Sullenberger, C., in *Horizon*, 'How to avoid mistakes in surgery', BBC2, first broadcast 21 March 2013
7. Kerr, J., *Legacy*, Constable and Robinson, London (2013)
8. Peters, T., *Thriving On Chaos: Handbook for a Management Revolution*, Knopf, New York (1987)

Chapter 5

1. Hall, B., *Team Spirit*, Adlard Coles Nautical, London (2012)
2. Hartley, S.R., *Two Lengths of the Pool: Sometimes the Simplest Ideas Have the Greatest Impact*, Be World Class, Arkendale, UK (2013)
3. Woodward, C., *Winning!*, Hodder and Stoughton, London (2004), p. 172
4. Hall, B., *Team Spirit*, Adlard Coles Nautical, London (2012)

5. Ibid

6. Sanford, N., *The American College*, Wiley, New York (1962); Sanford, N., *Self and Society: Social Change and Individual Development*, Atherton, New York (1966)

7. Ankersen, R., *The Gold Mine Effect: Unlocking The Essence of World Class Performance*, Rasmus Ankersen, London (2011)

8. Woodward, C., *Winning!*, Hodder and Stoughton, London (2004)

9. Surowiecki, J., *The Wisdom of Crowds: Why the Many Are Smarter Than the Few*, Little, Brown, London (2004)

10. Asch, S., *Social Psychology*, Prentice Hall, Englewoods Cliffs, NJ (1952)

11. Sullenberger, C., in *Horizon*, 'How to avoid mistakes in surgery', BBC2, first broadcast 21 March 2013

12. Kerr, J., *Legacy*, Constable and Robinson, London (2013)

13. Woodward, C., *Winning!*, Hodder and Stoughton, London (2004)

14. Ornstein, D., 'Crystal Palace: How Tony Pulis achieved Premier League survival', BBC Sport, 2 May 2014. Available online http://www.bbc.co.uk/sport/0/football/27253266 (accessed 5 July 2014)

15. Hall, B., *Team Spirit*, Adlard Coles Nautical, London (2012)

16. Hartley, S.R., *Peak Performance Every Time*, Routledge, London (2011)

Chapter 6

1. Hartley, S.R., *How To Shine; Insights into Unlocking your Potential from Proven Winners*, Capstone, Chichester (2012)

2. Woodrow, F. and Acland, S., *Elite!: The Secrets to Exceptional Leadership and Performance*, Elliott and Thompson, London (2012)

3. Hall, B., *Team Spirit*, Adlard Coles Nautical, London (2012)

4. Surowiecki, J., *The Wisdom of Crowds: Why the Many Are Smarter Than the Few*, Little, Brown, London (2004)

5. Woodward, C., *Winning!*, Hodder and Stoughton, London (2004)

6. Hall, B., *Team Spirit*, Adlard Coles Nautical, London (2012)

7. Hickson, M., 'Leadership From The Front Line', *Leadership in the 21st Century* (2013) pp. 8–9

8. Tzu, S., *The Art of War: The Oldest Military Treatise in the World* (1910), trans. Lionel Giles, Kessinger Publishing, Whitefish, MT (2010)

9. Burchard, B., 'What great leaders actually do', Brendon Burchard

YouTube Channel. Available online, https://www.youtube.com/user/BrendonBurchard?v=6SOTBHAcLV4 (accessed 8 August 2014)

10. Sinek, S., *Start With Why*, Portfolio Penguin, London (2011)
11. Trimble, V., *Overnight Success: FedEx and Frederick Smith, Its Renegade Creator*, Crown, New York (1993)
12. Tu, K., *Superteams*, Portfolio Penguin, London (2012)
13. Hall, B., *Team Spirit*, Adlard Coles Nautical, London (2012)
14. Woodrow, F. and Acland, S., *Elite!: The Secrets to Exceptional Leadership and Performance*, Elliott and Thompson, London (2012)
15. Hall, B., *Team Spirit*, Adlard Coles Nautical, London (2012)
16. Walters, C., 'Gregg Popovich on leadership and empowerment', Lean Blitz, 10 March 2014. Available online, http://leanblitzconsulting.com/2014/03/gregg-popovich-leadership-empowerment/
17. Welch, J. and Welch, S., 'How to Think Like a Leader', LinkedIn, 8 July 2013. Available online, https://www.linkedin.com/pulse/article/20130708115451–86541065-how-to-think-like-a-leader (accessed 10 November 2014)
18. Tzu, L., *Tao Te Ching*, trans. Stephen Addiss and Stanley Lombardo, Hackett Publishing, Indianapolis, IN (1993)
19. DePree, M., *Leadership is an Art*, Crown Business, New York (1989)
20. Wilson, W.S., *Ideals of the Samurai*, Blackbelt Communications, Valencia, CA (1982)
21. Hickson, M., 'Leadership From The Front Line', *Leadership In The 21st Century* (2013) pp. 8–9

Chapter 7

1. Jarvis, N., 'What is a Culture', NYSED. Available online, http://www.p12.nysed.gov/ciai/socst/grade3/whatisa.html (accessed 20 August 2014)
2. Ibid
3. Collins, J.C., *Good to Great*, Random House, London (2001)
4. Babb, T., 'Sir David Brailsford's 20 lessons in leadership', HarringtonStarr.com. Available online, http://www.harringtonstarr.com/sir-david-brailsfords-20-lessons-leadership/ (accessed 22 August 2014)
5. Hughes, D., *How to Think Like Sir Alex Ferguson: The Business of Winning and Managing Success*, Aurum Press, London (2014)
6. Surowiecki, J., *The Wisdom of Crowds: Why the Many Are Smarter Than the Few*, Little Brown, London (2004)

7. Kerr, J. and Hartley, S.R., 'On ... All Black Culture', Be World Class TV. Available online, http://www.beworldclass.tv (accessed 5 November 2014)

8. Jones, C., 'British and Irish Lions: Sir Ian McGeechan: How to win a Test series', BBC Sport, 28 May 2013

9. Walshe, A., 'Creating a High Performance Environment At Red Bull', *Leaders USA*, June 2013

10. Hall, B., *Team Spirit*, Adlard Coles Nautical, London (2012)

Index